Cambridge Elements

Elements in Eighteenth-Century Connections
edited by
Eve Tavor Bannet
University of Oklahoma
Markman Ellis
Queen Mary University of London

NETWORKS OF RECEPTION IN THE EIGHTEENTH-CENTURY BRITISH PRESS AND LAURENCE STERNE

Mary Newbould
Kazimierz Wielki University

Shaftesbury Road, Cambridge CB2 8EA, United Kingdom

One Liberty Plaza, 20th Floor, New York, NY 10006, USA

477 Williamstown Road, Port Melbourne, VIC 3207, Australia

314–321, 3rd Floor, Plot 3, Splendor Forum, Jasola District Centre, New Delhi – 110025, India

103 Penang Road, #05–06/07, Visioncrest Commercial, Singapore 238467

Cambridge University Press is part of Cambridge University Press & Assessment, a department of the University of Cambridge.

We share the University's mission to contribute to society through the pursuit of education, learning and research at the highest international levels of excellence.

www.cambridge.org
Information on this title: www.cambridge.org/9781009663199

DOI: 10.1017/9781009238465

© Mary Newbould 2025

This publication is in copyright. Subject to statutory exception and to the provisions of relevant collective licensing agreements, no reproduction of any part may take place without the written permission of Cambridge University Press & Assessment.

When citing this work, please include a reference to the DOI 10.1017/9781009238465

First published 2025

A catalogue record for this publication is available from the British Library

ISBN 978-1-009-66319-9 Hardback
ISBN 978-1-009-23849-6 Paperback
ISSN 2632-5578 (online)
ISSN 2632-556X (print)

Cambridge University Press & Assessment has no responsibility for the persistence or accuracy of URLs for external or third-party internet websites referred to in this publication and does not guarantee that any content on such websites is, or will remain, accurate or appropriate.

For EU product safety concerns, contact us at Calle de José Abascal, 56, 1°, 28003 Madrid, Spain, or email eugpsr@cambridge.org

Networks of Reception in the Eighteenth-Century British Press and Laurence Sterne

Elements in Eighteenth-Century Connections

DOI: 10.1017/9781009238465
First published online: October 2025

Mary Newbould
Kazimierz Wielki University
Author for correspondence: Mary Newbould, mcn23@cam.ac.uk

Abstract: Criticism and creativity characterised literary reception in eighteenth-century Britain. The press – periodicals, newspapers, and magazines – harboured the reviewing cultures belonging to the emerging professionalisation of literary criticism. It also provided a highly fertile ground for creativity, including imitative items inspired by new publications, while critical reviews often incorporated parody. The press fostered experimentation among often anonymous reader-contributors, even while it facilitated the establishment of 'classic' works by recirculating well-known authors' names. Laurence Sterne's reception was energetically shaped by the interaction between critical and creative responses: the press played a major role in forging his status as an 'inimitable' author of note.

Keywords: reception, newspapers, magazines, adaptation, Laurence Sterne

© Mary Newbould 2025

ISBNs: 9781009663199 (HB), 9781009238496 (PB), 9781009238465 (OC)
ISSNs: 2632-5578 (online), 2632-556X (print)

Contents

1 Introduction: Networks of Reception   1
2 Reviewing Cultures   13
3 Excerpt Culture   26
4 Creative Reception   36
5 Conclusion: Creating Classics through the Press   59

   Bibliography   65

1 Introduction: Networks of Reception

Newspapers, periodicals, and magazines – which I collectively call 'the press' – provided the backbone of eighteenth-century news networks, of social and political life, and of literary, artistic, and creative activity; they also supplied the currency of sociable exchange.[1] As one magazine contributor wrote, they formed 'the truest pictures of the manners and principles of the times; we should consult them to discover the reigning foibles and fashions' and 'popular subjects'.[2] These publications responded to the immediacy of events, international and local, and provided a litmus-test venue for new cultural products entering the market.[3] Literary reception took the form of critical reviews, which were also strongly marked by creativity – many reviewers employed parodic humour and playful inventiveness to make their point.[4] These tendencies were magnified in the various forms of creative writing also published in the press, including imitative responses to new or popular works, through which numerous, often anonymous reader-creators channelled critical opinions, admiration, or pleasure, or capitalised on the fame of the latest publishing success.

This Element explores the reception of Laurence Sterne (1713–68), a pioneer of fiction in the mid-eighteenth century, as disseminated through the British press from 1760 to the 1820s.[5] Sterne offers a significant case study for understanding the press's wider role in shaping literary reception in this period. From the outset, his works attracted critical discourse and creative enterprises alike, a heterogeneous body of material known as 'Sterneana'. 1760 marks Sterne's rapid rise to fame with the publication of the first two volumes of his serialised work, *The Life and Opinions of Tristram Shandy, Gentleman* (1759–67). By 1820, Sterne's reception – now encompassing more instalments of *Tristram Shandy*, *A Sentimental Journey through France and Italy* (1768), sermons, and posthumous publications (most prominently, his correspondence) following his death in 1768 – had changed significantly, partly in tandem with shifting literary tastes. So, too, had the press. Although Jeremy Black voices scepticism towards 'crucial dates' in the history of British newspapers, press publications in all forms began to look and read differently during the early decades of the nineteenth century.[6] While this study covers a set time-span for feasibility, there is also a rationale for aligning noticeable modulations in Sterne's reception with those in press history; it also lays groundwork for further exploring these domains in future.

---

[1] Barker, *Newspapers*, pp. 10–11. [2] *Universal Museum*, 1 (January 1762), 25.
[3] Heyd, 'News Craze', 62–8. [4] Donoghue, *Fame Machine*, pp. 2–3.
[5] I also discuss selected Irish, French, and American titles. [6] Black, *English Press*, pp. ix–x.

'Of all the names of literary figures that appear in the columns of newspapers and magazines during the 1760's, none appears so often, over such an extended period of time, or with such a variety of praise and censure as that of Laurence Sterne', Alan B. Howes writes.[7] That presence continually emerged in reviews, allusions, passing references, advertisements, afterlives, fragmented stories, poems, essays, serialised fiction, and Sternean name-tags, which focused on Sterne specifically – consolidating an authorial brand forged by his celebrity – or which, opportunistically, had little to do with either author or work beyond a superficial link. Sterne's presence in the press shaped his reception as significantly as, if not more than, the numerous adaptations in book-form typically used to describe it. The press contributed materially towards establishing his complicated status as admirable yet subject to censure, as 'inimitable' yet widely imitated. He was increasingly recognised as an author of note who deserved attention in the growing industry of literary criticism, positioned alongside but also distinguished from other writers. The press provided a platform for the visibility and dissemination of the Sternean brand comparable with, but distinct from that available to his contemporaries. Sterne's case, as both atypical and characteristic of its time, in turn illustrates wider trends in newspapers, magazines, and periodicals, including how they catalysed the transition from popular success and celebrity to literary significance, even while they fostered cultures of anonymity.

Critical and Creative Networks

The eighteenth century witnessed the emergence of what might now be described as the professionalisation of literary criticism, facilitated by publications that reviewed new works, which took hold from the mid-century onwards with two major periodicals, Ralph Griffiths's *Monthly Review* (1749–1845) and the *Critical Review* (1756–1817), first edited by Tobias Smollett. Reviews appeared across numerous magazines and newspapers, too, with differing readerships and aims. Critical and creative modes frequently intermeshed in reviews, and in new items printed in the press.[8] For one, this was a particularly fertile era for the imaginative adaptations that saw popular and successful publications transformed into new forms in alternative contexts of reception.[9] Many of the best-known eighteenth-century novels experienced afterlives, across art forms and genres,[10] including Daniel Defoe's *Strange Surprizing Adventures of Robinson Crusoe* (1719);[11] Jonathan Swift's *Gulliver's Travels*

---

[7] Howes, *Yorick and the Critics*, p. 1.   [8] Elliott, *Theorizing Adaptation*, p. 35.
[9] Suarez, 'Business of Fiction', pp. 30–2.
[10] Fairer, 'Introduction', pp. xxvi–vii; Elliott, *Theorizing Adaptation*, pp. 42–58.
[11] Lipski, 'Introduction', pp. 1–6.

(1726);[12] and Samuel Richardson's *Pamela* (1740), a publishing phenomenon partly manifested in and spread through adaptations – a forerunner to Sterne's reception.[13] Within the creative and commercial economies of eighteenth-century literary cultures, these transferral practices – involving parody, imitation, pastiche, burlesque, and which could in turn fuel satirical or polemic aims[14] – recirculated and recycled existing materials in what David Brewer has described as a 'feedback loop' linking creators and consumers.[15] Brewer's model parallels Simone Murray's proposal for 'a *sociology* of adaptation' that takes into account modern-day 'institutional, commercial and legal frameworks' pertaining to the 'cultural circulation' of adaptations.[16] The aim here is to think in a comparable way about how textual materials intertwined within the distinctive contexts of the eighteenth-century press, a unique sociological pool of production and consumption, critical analysis and creation, in which adaptive processes prospered.

The popularity of afterlife was closely linked with demographic shifts in reading.[17] A rapidly expanding market of consumers benefited from rising literacy levels, although claims about widespread literacy should be treated with caution; many readers were nevertheless able to buy or to borrow printed works far more easily than previous generations. The financial motility especially enjoyed by the so-called middling classes, expanded printing networks, and diversified environments for accessing printed material accelerated and disseminated reading via circulating libraries, coffee houses, and booksellers' shops throughout London and across an extensive provincial system.[18] While books were inevitably significant in these contexts, apparently more ephemeral items, such as chapbooks and broadside ballads – and press publications – considerably expanded the printed matter available to disparate types of audience.[19] '"Ephemera" is not a *thing* but a classification', Paula McDowell writes, which galvanised in the later eighteenth century as 'a response to the commercialization of letters and the proliferation of print'.[20] Ephemeral press publications passed through multiple hands with a scale and rapidity of production and circulation that was not matched by books; the consequences for the spread of an author's work, or for the idea of an author – captured in a name and

---

[12] Cook, 'Further Voyages', pp. 192–4.   [13] Keymer and Sabor, *'Pamela'*, pp. 1–5.
[14] Hutcheon, *Theory of Adaptation*, pp. 4–9, pp. 16–17.
[15] Brewer, *Afterlife*, p. 6, p. 14. See also Barker, *Newspapers*, pp. 103–4.
[16] Murray, *Adaptation Industry*, p. 4.   [17] Williams, *Social Life*, p. 11.
[18] Ellis, 'Poetry and Civic Urbanism', pp. 52–4; Barker, *Newspapers*, p. 46; Raven, *Business of Books*, p. 91.
[19] Seager, 'The Novel's Afterlife', p. 112; Somers, *Ephemeral Print Culture*, pp. 3–8; Suarez, 'Business of Fiction', pp. 35–6.
[20] McDowell, 'Of Grubs and Other Insects', pp. 31–2.

labels attached to his or her writing – were considerable. The press was also as important in the 'shared reading' practices associated with books described by Abigail Williams.[21] Circulating libraries, for instance, which carried a range of printed materials, created what Mark Vareschi calls a network of 'virtual circulation' in which reader-consumers were intrinsically connected: without physically meeting, they shared in a common pool of reading matter.[22] For Brewer, this fashioned a form of 'sociability' that was 'almost wholly virtual', inviting an imaginative participation that was particularly conducive to literary afterlives.[23] The press facilitated the expansion and activity of these virtual communities of readers-creators in ways distinct from books:[24] as a mode of publication that relied and thrived on multi-sided input, the press's network of anonymous, unknown, and unnumbered readers and contributors provides perhaps the closest eighteenth-century parallel to present-day fora such as social media chatrooms or fan-fiction sites, as Margaret J. M. Ezell and Jennie Batchelor, among others, have suggested.[25]

These environments for harbouring anonymity jostled alongside an equally lively emergent celebrity culture in this period. Significant critical attention has been given to figures including David Garrick, Samuel Johnson, or Lady Mary Wortley Montagu.[26] Sterne, as we shall see, unexpectedly found a notorious fame that fed into both critical and creative reactions to his work, and which, Thomas Keymer suggests, Sterne adeptly manipulated.[27] His case richly demonstrates how celebrity culture fictionalises a public figure that is both allied to the reality of a person and a fabrication. The press fostered this image-making industry, as Uriel Heyd argues: 'Eighteenth-century readers were hungry for celebrity items, newspapers were happy to cater', which 'fame-seeking individuals' exploited.[28] The press nevertheless exerted a seemingly contradictory function: it marketed celebrity, but it also cultivated anonymity and obscurity; many who felt they might have a go at writing were liberated by creative fora where numerous nameless contributors could put their efforts into print – including those that responded creatively to celebrated authors or publications. Nevertheless, one outcome of this Element is that it reveals how, somewhat paradoxically, while the press fostered a democratising free-play of creativity among reader-contributors, it also served a significant role in canon formation. By giving prominence to certain works, or their authors, or both – including by

---

[21] Williams, *Social Life*, p. 7.   [22] Vareschi, *Everywhere and Nowhere*, p. 143.
[23] Brewer, *Afterlife*, p. 14. See also Newbould, '"[It] Were Wisdome It Selfe"', 165.
[24] Heyd, 'News Craze', 73–4.
[25] Ezell, *Early English Periodicals*, pp. 2–3; Batchelor, '"Connections"', 255–6, 259–61; Batchelor, *The 'Lady's Magazine'*, pp. 222–3, pp. 226–7; see also Powell, *Performing Authorship*, pp. 2–3.
[26] Jones and Joule (eds.), *Intimacy and Celebrity*, pp. 2–3.   [27] Keymer, 'Small Particles', p. 17.
[28] Heyd, 'Fifteen Lines of Fame', pp. 100–104.

publishing adaptations they inspired – the press helped to establish many writers' significance in literary history. It facilitated both academic canonicity and the 'social canon' in a dual motion that simultaneously centralised and decentralised celebrity works or authors, and which both promoted and obscured anonymous contributors.[29] A query underlying this case study is how far Laurence Sterne's evolving position as an author of note – and, increasingly, of 'classic' status – was dependent on his continual presence in reviews and creative reactions that fed into the tangled web of materials held by press publications. Although it lies beyond the scope of this Element to explore other contemporary authors in detail, it nevertheless prompts a running query that can be more fully addressed elsewhere regarding how distinctive or how typical Sterne's case was in these respects.

Approaching Sterne's presence in the press as participating in a network of original invention and creative adaptation, celebrity and obscurity, transience and lasting fame, helps to resituate the hierarchical assumptions that risk imposing biased value judgements on literary, and especially adaptive materials, and on the ephemeral outlets in which they appeared.[30] Qualitative evaluation necessarily forms part of any literary-critical enterprise, yet it is striking how accounts of Sterneana sometimes feel compelled to reinforce its worthlessness: one of the biggest collections (held at Cambridge University Library) was amassed by J. C. T. Oates, but he repeatedly dismissed its items as 'trivial', 'rubbish', 'tasteless and barren', 'lunatic', 'irredeemable twaddle', and so on.[31] Value judgements shift if we move away from thinking about adaptations as solely dependent upon an originary source, especially a famous one. Paul Goring highlights the drawbacks of '-ana'-oriented narratives, which can privilege an author-centric approach that too simply confirms notions of canonicity that were more nuanced in their own historical moment – although, he concludes, 'Sterneana' remains a useful critical term.[32] Beyond Sterne, Daniel Cook and Nicholas Seager suggest that, if we consider eighteenth-century adaptation in terms of 'mutual relations between "versions" of works' rather than of restrictive hierarchies, then we gain a richer picture of the period's cultural productivity.[33]

'Networks' provides one way of describing adaptive practices as part of a non-hierarchic environment of literary productivity, and of the patterns of criticism and creativity mapped across press publications explored here.[34] Franco Moretti's diagrams representing relations between literary works' character and plot elements, for instance, visualise a simultaneous bunching and dispersal of connecting

---

[29] Brewer, citing Franco Moretti, *Afterlife*, p. 17.   [30] Elliott, *Theorizing Adaptation*, pp. 43–4.
[31] Oates, *Shandyism*. See also Bandry, *Créations*, p. 7.
[32] Goring, 'Authorial Authority', 182–5.   [33] Cook and Seager, 'Introduction', p. 2.
[34] Goring, 'Network of Networks', p. 4.

nodes that concentrates on specific points but also decentralises any given node.[35] As Goring points out, Gilles Deleuze and Félix Guttari's now often-cited network theory similarly rejects the hierarchical implications of arborescence.[36] Their preference for the rhizome – a botanical term that describes an underground plant stem which can produce the roots and shoots of a new plant – posits a multinodal approach that situates the originary work as one among a cluster of creative products that feed off and into each other.[37] The metaphors Deleuze and Guttari develop – of a book as 'an assemblage ... in connection with other assemblages and in relation to other bodies without organs' – serve network theory and, in turn, the circulatory systems of adaptation, and of press publications.[38] As Black writes, eighteenth-century newspapers 'were part of a far from enclosed system of information', intersecting with 'printed matter, such as books and magazines, and unprinted matter, such as newsletters and merchants' correspondence'.[39] Network theories have also been assigned to Sterne's work – John Havard, for instance, uses 'social network analysis' to discuss the connections between Sterne's fiction and his politics[40] – and to Sterneana, as Goring shows.[41] The concept and motions of networks characterise the interactive relations belonging to Sterne's reception, and its aptness as a case study demonstrating how press publications embodied such generative exchanges.

'Brand Sterne' and the Press

Sterne was an unlikely candidate for celebrity.[42] He was middle-aged by the time he produced *Tristram Shandy* and *A Sentimental Journey* in the final decade of his life. Until 1760, he pursued the fairly typical career of a rural clergyman who had published two sermons and *A Political Romance* (1759), a short pamphlet satirising local clerical politics, which was suppressed; it nonetheless gave Sterne the taste for a type of comic writing that he developed in the first two volumes of *Tristram Shandy*.[43] Initially printed in York in December 1759 but distributed in London in January 1760, they promptly sold out. Sterne became an overnight success along with his book, and the first wave of 'Shandymania' took hold, manifested in critical reviews and imitative pieces – mostly pamphlets and items printed in the press.[44] They foregrounded the most distinctive Shandean traits: bawdy humour, innuendo, wide-ranging references to other authors and books, self-reflexive metafiction,

---

[35] Moretti, 'Network Theory', 84–6. [36] Goring, 'Authorial Authority', 183.
[37] Deleuze and Guttari, *Thousand Plateaus*, pp. 6–8; Goring, 'Authorial Authority', 193.
[38] Deleuze and Guttari, *Thousand Plateaus*, p. 5. See also Nicklas and Lindner, 'Adaptation', p. 2.
[39] Black, *English Press*, pp. 87–8. [40] Havard, 'Only Disconnect?', p. 268, pp. 277–8.
[41] Goring, 'Authorial Authority', 183–5, 193–4. [42] Cash, *Later Years*, pp. 1–21.
[43] Sterne, *Miscellaneous Writings*, p. xviii.
[44] For in-depth discussions, see Bandry, *Créations*; Bosch, *Labyrinths*; Newbould, *Adaptations*.

inventive typography, graphic features, and memorable characters.[45] Sterne quickly capitalised upon his unexpected fame by publishing two volumes of his own sermons in May 1760 under the provocative title *The Sermons of Mr. Yorick*, the borrowed name of *Tristram Shandy*'s fictional parson. Success bred ambition: two more volumes of *Tristram Shandy* appeared the following year, then two further instalments of two volumes each, until a final, lone volume 9 appeared in 1767. *Tristram Shandy*'s serialised publication drove an energetically interactive dialogue with its critics and imitators.[46]

A Sentimental Journey's reception followed a different pattern. Only two volumes of an originally promised four were published in February 1768, as Sterne died shortly afterwards in March. It was well-received by critics, who admired its moralistic pathos, and it inspired posthumous adaptations that responded to the work's apparently defining feature, sensibility, but also to its complex handling by Sterne. From more straightforwardly sentimentalised fragments and fuller-length works, to pathetic songs and affective images, to innuendo-laced continuations and erotic illustrations, *A Sentimental Journey* stimulated diverse responses that engaged with the text's own malleability, but also with the by-then wider array of materials, including posthumous publications, comprising what was meant by 'Sterne' as a label: an eventual seven volumes of sermons, correspondence, and shorter works packaged up with the letters, including Sterne's memoirs, *A Political Romance*, and his 'Rabelaisian Fragment'. Further complexity emerges given that, although this Element focuses on Sterne's early reception in the British Isles, his work has consistently been read, translated, and adapted across the European continent, North America, and further afield, as reflected in global press outlets that, like British counterparts, harboured wide-ranging critical and creative responses to Sterne.[47]

Opinions continually oscillated between disapproval and enthusiastic praise, reflecting how far readers remained divided about what to make of Sterne's eclectic output. The task for readers and critics of making sense of Sterne was made more challenging by the extent to which the semi-fictional identity of the author himself was enmeshed in the production and the perception of his written output. 'Brand Sterne' – comprising, in part, a cluster of lexical terms which rapidly emerged across reviews and creative responses – to a degree helped to codify this perplexing author and his mixed output, while simultaneously acknowledging his commercial success and celebrity status.[48] In a comparable way to the 'processes of repetition and virtualization' that Vareschi notes of

---

[45] Keymer, *Sterne*, pp. 4–8.
[46] Bandry, *Créations*, p. 245; Keymer, *Sterne*, pp. 85–110, pp. 121–49.
[47] See Voogd and Neubauer (eds.), *Reception*.
[48] The coinage 'brand Sterne' recalls Andrew Pettegree, *Brand Luther*.

Defoe's *Moll Flanders* and *Roxana*, whereby their titular names were repeatedly recirculated but increasingly detached from 'the physical book and content', Sterne's writing, and his own name, were subject to a labelling seemingly attached to author and work, but which was also a fictive construct;[49] 'After all, a *brand* is not a product in its own right, but rather is a sign or, even more concretely, an icon that embodies an identity myth.'[50] Created by critical impetuses and commercial interests, the Sternean label fed off Sterne's celebrity status and served ostensibly to make author and work more easily identifiable, but also marketable – which spin-offs readily exploited.[51] The press was an adept mechanism for advertising and recirculating this sellable brand.

The labelling belonging to Sterne's reception in part confirms the dynamics of the literary market in ways that align with Catherine Gallagher's examination of 'nothingness and disembodiment' in women's writing of the long eighteenth century: she deliberately chooses known, named authors – not 'ignored, silenced, erased, or anonymous women' – to explore the workings of a patriarchal marketplace.[52] As a named, male, white, Anglican clergyman, 'Sterne' was an identifiable authorial signifier that carried establishment weight – but also certain expectations that, if they were considered unmet, supplied critical ballast (the clash between his clerical and fiction-writing professions, for instance). The brand label seemed to confirm success, commercial and popular, but its very fabrication as a 'sign' that embodied a 'myth' challenged straightforwardly authoritative authorship. For Brewer, 'reconstructing' how the names of key authors were used as signpost-labels can better access 'a then-pervasive conception of authorship ... the idea that authors *qua* authors were not fully human', and that they (and their works) could 'operate more like counters to be pushed around than straightforward indices pointing toward specific biographical individuals'.[53] These disembodied conceptions of authorship both confirmed and contested the canonical associations of authorial (celebrity) naming.[54] Sterne inhabited the 'posture' of his brand to assert his position as a literary celebrity, but the interactive nature of literary reception in general, and of Sterne's in particular, made any such assertions of self-image highly volatile in the entanglement of genuine works, critical reviews, and creative reactions, which endured after Sterne's death.[55]

Sterneana in the form of books, pamphlets, illustrations, artworks, and realia has received sustained attention; however, Sterne's reception in periodicals, newspapers, and magazines has been examined less consistently or thoroughly,

---

[49] Vareschi, *Everywhere and Nowhere*, pp. 130–1. [50] Braber et al., 'Introduction', p. 11.
[51] Suarez, 'Business of Fiction', pp. 30–1. [52] Gallagher, *Nobody's Story*, p. xiii, p. xviii.
[53] Brewer, 'Tactility', 195–6. [54] Powell, *Performing Authorship*, pp. 29–30.
[55] Braber et al., 'Introduction', p. 21.

with a few important exceptions.[56] Examples have tended to be used as illustrative, ancillary, or in passing, with studies predominantly based on albeit invaluable book-title bibliographies such as the *English Short Title Catalogue* (*ESTC*) presenting skewed reception histories.[57] Sterne was present to eighteenth-century readers far more continuously, and variedly, through press publications than books. Alan B. Howes's 1974 *Critical Heritage* volume has long provided an important anthology of this material, with excerpts from Sterne's works, contemporary reviews, Sterneana, and private correspondence.[58] There are inevitable limitations to the necessary selectiveness of extracts, and to the wider contexts excluded by an excerpt. Not only what, but how a Sterne-related item greeted the eye of an eighteenth-century reader informs understanding of the period's press cultures, but also the simultaneous significance and insignificance of Sterne within a vaster network of associations.

What Was 'the Press'?

So far, I have used the terms 'periodical', 'newspaper', and 'magazine' interchangeably under the broad term 'the press', whereas they were, of course, distinctive types of publication, even if they shared several features in common.[59]

Periodicals flourished in the later seventeenth and early eighteenth centuries. Published weekly, and sometimes on more days per week, periodicals' contents were eclectic, compiling news, literary miscellanies, and essays often penned by pseudonymous authors, 'Mr. Spectator' being perhaps the most famous eidolon of Joseph Addison and Richard Steele's *Spectator* (1711–14).[60] Periodicals commented on, and in turn shaped, public opinions and social practices, and literary and artistic cultures as they evolved. Although a strict chronological or generic account is difficult to establish, during the decades explored by this Element periodicals had ceded in significance;[61] while periodicals are an important repository for the critical reviews discussed here, newspapers and magazines were more populous, and the most fertile location for creative responses to Sterne's work.

There were thousands of newspapers in this period, some short-lived, some still running today, produced in highly volatile political and social contexts.[62] Newspapers were usually printed daily, twice or more a week, or weekly.

---

[56] Howes, *Yorick and the Critics*; Anne Bandry-Scubbi's work, see Bibliography; Donoghue, *Fame Machine*; Goring, 'The Evolution'.
[57] Raven, *Publishing Business*, pp. 53–4. [58] See also Howes, *Yorick and the Critics*.
[59] Barker, *Newspapers*, p. 2. [60] Ezell, *Early English Periodicals*, pp. 3–5.
[61] Ezell, *Early English Periodicals*, pp. 3–8; Pettegree, *Invention*, pp. 270–86; Powell, *Performing Authorship*, pp. 7–8.
[62] Ferdinand, *Benjamin Collins*, pp. 17–19; Pettegree, *Invention*, p. 308; Raven, *Business of Books*, pp. 258–62.

London was the seed-bed of titles during our period of interest, but the British Isles as a whole enjoyed a very lively newspaper trade concentrated in major cities – Dublin, Edinburgh, York, Newcastle – while smaller towns and cities had provincial papers of their own, reporting on local news but also reprinting items found in the London papers, a recirculation aided by a developed postal service.[63] Similarly, as Black explains, 'London newspapers took a lot of information from foreign and other London newspapers'.[64] National and international news-sharing networks were sophisticated and complex.[65] Sharing was also common among newspaper readers, although that readership is difficult to determine in terms of gender, class, profession, or economic means.[66] Alongside the news usually printed in columns across an average of four sides of broadsheet, newspapers were a 'disorganised jumble of information and misinformation, opinion, and advertisements'.[67] They comprised theatrical bills; notices for lost and found objects and persons (anything ranging from banknotes to children); advertisements for books, local services, and consumer products, occasionally accompanied by wood-block illustrations; letters from readers; and creative pieces – poems, short essays, and fragmentary narratives, which were sometimes serialised across several issues.[68]

Magazines shared many features in common with periodicals;[69] likewise, Andrew Prescott suggests, 'the distinction between [newspapers and magazines] has been overstated', and there were as many correspondences as differences.[70] Magazines had some comparable elements, including news items and advertisements, but they often carried longer reviews than those found in newspapers (of literary publications, of theatrical performances), more contributors' correspondence, and longer creative pieces – short stories, serialised essays, and fiction – as well as poetry.[71] Magazines were published less frequently than newspapers (usually monthly), placed a greater emphasis on aesthetic qualities, and cost more to produce and to buy.[72] This was, Gillian Williamson writes in discussing the *Gentleman's Magazine*, a fiercely competitive market, where titles vied for readers' attention.[73] Illustrations were selling-points: they accompanied fictional pieces, and encompassed maps, diagrams, portraits, and plates, of botanical studies or women's fashion, for instance.[74] It is

---

[63] Barker, *Newspapers*, p. 29; Ferdinand, *Benjamin Collins*, pp. 5–22; Goring, 'Network of Networks', p. 8; Raven, *Publishing Business*, pp. 163–4.
[64] Black, *English Press*, pp. 87–8.   [65] Goring, 'Network of Networks', pp. 3–4, pp. 11–12.
[66] Barker, *Newspapers*, pp. 46–51.   [67] Heyd, 'News Craze', 75.
[68] Black, *English Press*, pp. 26–7, pp. 51–2.
[69] Powell, *Performing Authorship*, pp. 15–16, pp. 22–3.
[70] Prescott, 'Searching for Dr. Johnson', p. 65.   [71] Williams, *Social Life*, pp. 233–4.
[72] Black, *English Press*, pp. 104–8.   [73] Williamson, *British Masculinity*, p. 1.
[74] Anderson, 'Magazine Illustration', 79–80.

important not to delineate types of publication along simplistic gendered lines: while sometimes considered more 'masculine', periodicals were an important vehicle for women's work, for instance,[75] and newspaper-reading was popular among women.[76] Nevertheless, magazines were a significant component in the burgeoning domain of women's publishing. Several titles were run by women and overtly marketed themselves for a female readership,[77] such as Caroline Amelia Stanhope's *Lady's Magazine* (1759–63) and Charlotte Lennox's *Lady's Museum* (1760–61).[78] While they published contributions from male authors and reached a male readership they supplied a space for publication that some contributors might not have easily found elsewhere.[79] As Batchelor has shown, the *Lady's Magazine* (1770–1837) – distinct from Stanhope's earlier *Lady's Magazine* – was one important platform for new creative talent.[80]

In both magazines and newspapers many aspiring authors were encouraged to contribute by the shield provided by anonymity – which was widely practised in the eighteenth century but saw a notable increase from the 1770s onwards,[81] like its bedfellow, pseudonymity; Sam Sarcasm, Antigallicus, Swift's Ghost, and, indeed, Tristram Shandy were all used as sign-offs.[82] Name-evasion provided one mechanism by which reader-contributors across a wide spectrum could be enticed to share in the sense of community press cultures created. Ezell establishes a continuous line between earlier periodical essayists such as Addison and Steele and Samuel Johnson, writing in the *Rambler* mid-century, to show how a 'different type of relationship between readers and authors' emerged that 'rejected the dynamics of participatory literary culture for creating content'.[83] However, magazines clearly thrived on just such a dynamic: readers 'imagined themselves to be active participants in the magazine's print community', Batchelor suggests.[84] For Heyd, similarly, emergent celebrity culture 'saw newspapers ... shaping their readership in an interactive way'.[85] Furthermore, unsigned pieces could facilitate collaborative or multi-authored items, especially in the contexts of serialisation, further liberating the possibilities for creativity;[86] the connection between an unnamed item and a named author, which adaptation

---

[75] Batchelor and Powell, 'Introduction', pp. 1–2.   [76] Heyd, 'News Craze', 70–1.
[77] Batchelor and Powell, 'Introduction', pp. 5–6.
[78] *The Lady's Museum Project*, https://ladysmuseum.com/. 'Caroline Amelia Stanhope' was probably fictitious, possibly a pseudonym used by Oliver Goldsmith (Ballaster et al., *Women's Worlds*, pp. 64–5); Batchelor queries that identification, *The 'Lady's Magazine'*, pp. 39–40.
[79] Fergus, *Provincial Readers*, pp. 200–206.
[80] Batchelor, *The 'Lady's Magazine'*, pp. 3–4; Batchelor, '"Connections"', 249; Batchelor and Powell, 'Introduction', pp. 7–8.
[81] Vareschi, *Everywhere and Nowhere*, pp. 5–10.   [82] Bandry-Scubbi, 'The Visitor', 291–2.
[83] Ezell, *Early English Periodicals*, p. 2.
[84] Batchelor, *The 'Lady's Magazine'*, p. 52; Batchelor, '"Connections"', 250–1.
[85] Heyd, 'Fifteen Lines of Fame', p. 103.   [86] Suarez, 'Business of Fiction', pp. 32–3.

and celebrity cultures facilitated, fuelled the feeling of participation in a literary community which these press publications nurtured.

The flourishing culture of serialisation – which, James Raven writes, even extended to advertising[87] – alongside the brevity of many items was well suited to what Nicholas Seager calls 'a new temporal sense' in reading habits that increasingly favoured 'fragmentary, periodic modes of reading and with episodic, additive, and disposable forms of narrative'.[88] Recent discussions of time in this period point towards how textual material then, as now, was increasingly consumed in more bite-sized portions – snippets that seemed better suited to increasingly busy and time-bound lives, or which felt busy because increasingly time-bound. Christina Lupton asks: 'if work time, clock time, and instrumental time use become signatures of life for common people in the eighteenth century, most of whom still work unthinkably long hours, how are we to explain the hours they sat with books in this period?'[89] Perhaps paradoxically, her argument also pertains to apparently less time-consuming reading materials such as newspapers, magazines, and periodicals. The press catered for the felt busyness Lupton describes, not only by supplying digestible nuggets of content, all mouldable to constrained time-pockets, but by pulling reader-consumers into their network of contribution and creativity. Reading, but also writing became more feasible tasks when broken down into manageable chunks.[90] The encouragement to contribute creative fragments forged a sense of virtually connected communities sustained across a network of print publications.

Newspapers and magazines, then, if distinct, shared similarities as multi-authored, multi-producer, collaborative print events. They involved the labour of typesetters, printers, distributors; of financing proprietors, with notable creative control; of paper-sewers, illustrators, and engravers (for magazines); and of the countless contributors who expected no named acknowledgement or remuneration, the only reward being the pleasure of seeing their work go into print, and of participating in the sprawling community of reader-contributors that kept these publications alive.[91] Sterne's work and its critical and creative responses were discernible elements in this context, in an ever-increasing network of reference-points related to, but detachable from Sterne.

Digital resources facilitate exploring this material in ways unavailable to previous generations of scholars (including Howes).[92] This study, for instance, has drawn on *Adam Matthew Digital*, *British Library Newspapers*, the *Seventeenth and Eighteenth Century Burney Newspapers Collection*, *British Newspaper Archive*, and *British Periodicals 1 and 2*, alongside *Eighteenth*

---

[87] Raven, 'Serial Advertisement', p. 103.   [88] Seager, 'The Novel's Afterlife', p. 113.
[89] Lupton, *Reading*, p. 5.   [90] Williams, *Social Life*, pp. 76–7.
[91] Batchelor, *The 'Lady's Magazine'*, p. 141.   [92] Goring, 'Network of Networks', pp. 21–2.

Century Collections Online (*ECCO*), *Google Books*, and *HathiTrust Digital Library*, which carry several magazines. These datasets complement Sterne-specific digital projects and heritage-sector sites.[93] As rapidly as online resources are praised for the research opportunities they provide, they are condemned for their drawbacks: limited accessibility, paywalls, image reproduction quality, and unreliable search functions.[94] However, consulting both physical copies of original materials and the vast array available online, ranging across multiple types of publication, and metropolitan, provincial, and international titles, produces a much richer and more challenging account of Sterne's reception, and what it reveals about the press's role in wider eighteenth-century literary history.

2 Reviewing Cultures

Reviews printed in periodicals, newspapers, and magazines significantly shaped the contemporary reception of new publications, and contributed towards enhancing, or demoting, the status of a work or its creator. This publicity fuelled the industry of imitations of popular publications, which were in turn subject to review themselves, keeping alive awareness of the publication that had inspired them in a revolving loop of critical response and creativity.

The brief span of Sterne's publishing activity was mediated by emergent professional criticism, which progressively consolidated Sterne's authorial standing.[95] For Frank Donoghue, 'Laurence Sterne offers perhaps the most valuable case study of a mid-eighteenth-century literary career', exemplifying the relationship between the period's reviewing and celebrity cultures.[96] The perception of Sterne, author and works, nevertheless underwent considerable change throughout the 1760s and subsequently; reviews played a significant part in determining his status at a time when reviewing culture itself was being defined by the print publications through which it circulated. Comments on and about Sterne spread across the press, beyond the major periodicals – notably the *Critical Review* and the *Monthly Review* – perpetuating dissent, admiration, and pleasure, while developing an increasingly recognisable critical vocabulary to describe this perplexing author and his work: humane, pathetic, indecent, humorous. The dominant watchword of 'inimitability' sustained a continual refrain.[97] Sterne's reviewers were stylistically inventive, often parodying his manner, bringing seemingly more objective critical reviews and imitative

---

[93] See Newbould and Williams, 'Literary Adaptation'; *Laurence Sterne and Sterneana*, https://cudl.lib.cam.ac.uk/collections/sterne/1; The Laurence Sterne Trust, www.laurencesternetrust.org.uk/.
[94] Prescott, 'Searching for Dr. Johnson', pp. 59–65.   [95] Donoghue, *Fame Machine*, p. 58.
[96] Donoghue, *Fame Machine*, p. 56.   [97] Howes, *Yorick and the Critics*, pp. 57–60.

Sterneana into dialogue with Sterne's texts, and with each other. Although the 1760s saw a frenzied period of creative and critical activity – by Sterne, and by his critics and imitators – which capitalised on *Tristram Shandy*'s initial burst of fame and ensuing serialisation, the sermons, *A Sentimental Journey*, and posthumous publications added moss to the rolling stone of 'brand Sterne' as it evolved over the ensuing decades.

Tristram Shandy and *The Sermons of Mr. Yorick*

The first review of *Tristram Shandy*, by William Kenrick, was published anonymously in the *Monthly Review* in January 1760; mostly appreciative, it positions Sterne's work against the landscape of contemporaneous novelistic fiction, while highlighting the logical inconsistencies of a first-person narrative related by a character who 'is still an embrio'.[98] The *Monthly Review*'s proprietor, Ralph Griffiths, also ran the shorter-lived *Grand Magazine*; its February issue reprinted a curtailed version of Kenrick's review, a practice of borrowing between publications that was common in the period.[99] Indeed, Kenrick's review also reappeared in the *Scots Magazine* in April.[100] The short notice in Tobias Smollett's *Critical Review* singles out *Tristram Shandy*'s characters as successfully drawn.[101]

Critical assessment of Sterne's work mingled with a more playful approach towards both *Tristram Shandy* and the art of reviewing: parody drew attention to the features on which the reviewer wished to focus, such as the *London Magazine*'s dash-heavy 'Oh rare Tristram Shandy!—Thou very sensible—humourous—pathetick—humane—unaccountable!—what shall we call thee?—Rabelais, Cervantes, What?'[102] Parodic reviews chimed with the imitative pamphlets caught in the initial flurry of Shandymania; they illuminate what attracted Sterne's earliest critics, and how mimicry formed part of the interchange that would develop between readers, texts, and author.[103] They, too, were subject to critical assessments that sometimes quoted excerpts, recirculating the Shandean parody. The *Universal Review* targets the well-known *Clockmakers Outcry Against the Author of the Life and Opinions of Tristram Shandy* to attack competitor publications: it peddles 'downright Billingsgate, not unlike what the Critical or Monthly Reviews discharge in their periodical hashes'.[104] This

---

[98] [Kenrick], *Monthly Review*, 21 (December 1759, appendix; January 1760), 56–71.
[99] *Grand Magazine* (February 1760), 92–3. Black, *English Press*, p. 96; Goring, 'Network of Networks', pp. 5–7.
[100] *Scots Magazine*, 22 (April 1760), 223–4.   [101] *Critical Review*, 9 (January 1760), 73–4.
[102] *London Magazine*, 29 (February 1760), 111–12.
[103] Bandry, *Créations*, p. 10; Bosch, *Labyrinth*, pp. 101–9.
[104] *Universal Review* (May 1760), 293–4.

pamphlet's text was recirculated in the lengthy quotations published in reviews in the *Monthly Review* in May and the *Grand Magazine* in June.[105] The *Critical Review* critiques contemporary book-market practices in its account of *Explanatory Remarks upon the Life and Opinions of Tristram Shandy* by 'Kunastrokius': even as early as April, 'we are tired with the encomiums bestowed on Tristram Shandy by those half-witted critics, who echo public report from coffee-house to coffee-house'.[106]

Sterne, as his letters show, initially enjoyed how these pamphlets fuelled his success, but quickly tired of those whom the *Monthly Review* calls 'miserable Pamphleteers' who 'prostitute their talents' in such pieces as *Tristram Shandy at Ranelagh*.[107] These publications and their reviews nevertheless promoted awareness of Sterne, keeping name-tags associated with his publications alive in the public consciousness. Already in early 1760, the difficulty of imitating Sterne became a running thread. In June, the *Critical Review* declares of one pamphlet that it is 'The most stupid, unmeaning, silly attempt to humour, that ever insulted the public curiosity after every thing that bears the name of Shandy'.[108] For the *Monthly Review*, 'few can contend with Mr. St— for wit, yet every Scribbler can write asterisms, and make blanks for baudy words', while *Tristram Shandy in a Reverie* is 'All froth and folly: imitating Mr. Sterne's manner' but going 'awry'.[109] A tangle of originality and imitation, criticism and creativity, was further entwined when newspaper advertisements for Sterne and for Sterneana were located next to each other, visually suggesting cross-fertilisation.[110]

Whether named, pseudonymous, or anonymous, authorial identity was woven into the reception of new works.[111] Early reviews' emphasis on the 'Shandy' name nevertheless suggests the significance of labelling in distinguishing authentic productions from fabrications. By June, Sterne was well known to be *Tristram Shandy*'s author; that his soubriquet or suggestive elisions appear in these reviews as often as his own name – 'Mr. St—', 'Mr. Shandy', '*Shandy*' – contributed towards the impression that his emerging brand was deliberately quixotic. 'Yorick' was soon added to the mix. The identification was made as early as February 1760 when the *London Chronicle* reprinted *Tristram Shandy*'s description of Yorick, announcing that '*The following Character of a Person called* YORICK ... *is by some supposed to be the*

---

[105] *Monthly Review*, 22 (May 1760), 436–37; *Grand Magazine*, 3 (June 1760), 316–17.
[106] *Critical Review*, 9 (April 1760), 319–20.
[107] *Monthly Review*, 22 (June 1760), 548. See Donoghue, *Fame Machine*, p. 57.
[108] *Critical Review*, 9 (June 1760), 493.   [109] *Monthly Review*, 22 (June 1760), 548–9.
[110] Brandtzæg, Newbould, and Williams, 'Advertising Sterne's Novels', 37–42.
[111] Newbould, '"[It] Were Wisdome It Selfe"', 166–7.

Character of the Author, as he himself chuses it should be exhibited',[112] a claim readvertised in the *Public Ledger*.[113] 'Yorick' was to become an even more popular pseudonym for Sterne than 'Tristram Shandy'. John Hill's pseudo-biography, '*Anecdotes of a Fashionable Author, in a Letter to the Ladies Magazine*', blended these identities in Stanhope's *Lady's Magazine* in April 1760, asking 'Who has not read the life of Tristram Shandy [?] … who will grudge five minutes and a half to know something of poor Yorick?'[114] These 'Anecdotes' were quickly reprinted in newspapers, including the *London Chronicle* and the *Newcastle General Magazine*, as non-London titles entered into conversation with literary phenomena in the capital.[115]

Perhaps, in probably reading such pieces, Sterne consolidated an existing plan for publishing his own sermons – or even got the idea for labelling their authorship – for, from mid-April onwards, advertisements for *The Sermons of Mr. Yorick* were juxtaposed with 'Published by the Rev. Mr. STERNE, Prebendary of York'.[116] Two volumes of sermons duly appeared in May 1760, with a frontispiece engraved by François Ravenet of the portrait Joshua Reynolds had painted of this new celebrity in March-April 1760.[117] For Claire Squires, 'Brand images, particularly author brand images, work towards creating associations in readers' minds' concerning author and book.[118] Similarly, in the eighteenth century, authorial portrait frontispieces – including 'counterfeit' ones – exerted nominalist and commercial clout, as Janine Barchas describes.[119] Reviewers disapproved, the *Monthly Review*'s Owen Ruffhead observing that 'the indecency of such an assumed character' risked derailing the sermons' genuine value: 'For who is this *Yorick?*'; the name recalls both 'a *Jester*' and 'an obscene Romance.—', meaning *Tristram Shandy*.[120] 'Animadversions on Tristram Shandy', printed in the *Grand Magazine* in June 1760, comically calls '*Tristy*' a 'jolly dog of a divine' who talks bawdy: '—smoke the parson!—'.[121] The infamous '****', indicating Uncle Toby's euphemism for his sister-in-law's intimate body-parts, replaces Sterne's name in the caption of an engraving of Reynolds's portrait. These 'four stars' became a visual symbol of the authorial brand, especially to satirise Sternean innuendo.[122] Although 'a branded author' might manipulate the 'difference between posture (one's self-image) and persona

---

[112] *London Chronicle*, 485, 2–5 February 1760, 124–5; also *Royal Female Magazine* (February 1760), 56–60.
[113] *Public Ledger*, 22, 6 February 1760, 4. [114] *Lady's Magazine* (April 1760), 337–43.
[115] *London Chronicle*, 524, 3–6 May 1760, 434–5; *Newcastle General Magazine* (May 1760), 265–9; Howes, *Critical Heritage*, p. 73.
[116] For instance, *London Chronicle*, 518, 19–22 April 1760, 5.
[117] Cash, *Later Years*, pp. 30–2. [118] Squires, *Marketing Literature*, p. 89.
[119] Barchas, *Graphic Design*, pp. 19–21. [120] *Monthly Review*, 22 (May 1760), 422–31.
[121] *Grand Magazine*, 3 (April 1760), 194–8.
[122] Bosch, *Labyrinth*, pp. 104–6; Newbould, *Adaptations*, pp. 156–8, p. 194.

(one's image in the eyes of others)' to control the narrative of their own reception,[123] Sterne's public persona was partly self-determined yet contingent on the volatile contexts of his works' reception.

The reviews of and reprinted excerpts from Sterne's texts and Sterneana recirculated in the pages of press publications in early 1760, indeed, created a brand image that adhered in the public imagination. This undoubtedly fuelled new Shandy-type ventures, but which were very quickly anchored to the idea of what the authentic (if problematic) Sternean label encompassed. A spurious 'volume III' of *Tristram Shandy* (published anonymously by John Carr) appeared in October 1760, anticipating Sterne's the following year, but was quickly denounced by the *Public Advertiser*.[124] 'Not genuine.', the *Monthly Review* starkly notes.[125] Nonetheless, the same periodical affirms in December that *A Supplement to the Life of Tristram Shandy* 'really has the knack of talking ... in the vein of the true and original Tristram Shandy himself'.[126] For the *Critical Review*, it is 'devoid of wit, humour, sense, and erudition', especially compared with *Yorick's Meditations on Various Important and Interesting Subjects*, produced by the same pseudo-Shandy earlier that year.[127] 'Voici encore une copie du fameux *Tristram*', and probably not the last, the *Annales typographiques* noted of this piece in July 1760, as Sterne's reception, partly mediated by imitative 'copies', spread to France.[128]

A lively game of tag between reviewers, imitators, and 'authentic' author ensued, and played a role in *Tristram Shandy*'s own development.[129] When the real volumes 3 and 4 appeared in January 1761 Sterne ruefully rebuked '—— You Messrs. the Monthly Reviewers!' who 'cut and slash my jerkin' in hostile reviews.[130] *Tristram Shandy*'s evolutive appearance exposed Sterne to an evaluation subject to change: the new volumes were generally deemed less successful. In February the *British Magazine*'s short notice mimically asserts: 'it had been well for the father, and perhaps for the public, that [Mrs Shandy] had remained all her life un—'.[131] The *Monthly Review*'s Ruffhead, again, regretted the periodical's promotion of 'the first two volumes of this extravagant work' given the second instalment, and the 'indecently' published sermons.[132] The *Scots Magazine* compounded the critique in March by reprinting the

---

[123] Braber et al., 'Introduction', p. 22.   [124] Bandry-Scubbi, 'Les faux volumes', 26, 30.
[125] *Monthly Review*, 23 (October 1760), 327.   [126] *Monthly Review*, 23 (December 1760), 522.
[127] *Critical Review*, 10 (December 1760), 485.   [128] *Annales typographiques*, 2 (July 1760), 57.
[129] Bandry, *Créations*, p. 245; Bandry-Scubbi, 'Sterne recyclé', 13–14; Bosch, *Labyrinth*, pp. 34–6.
[130] Sterne, *Tristram Shandy*, vol. 1, pp. 190–1.
[131] *British Magazine*, 2 (February 1761), 98. See also Cash, *Later Years*, pp. 88–9.
[132] *Monthly Review*, 24 (February 1761), 101–16.

Monthly Review's accounts of volumes 3 and 4 and of *The Sermons of Mr. Yorick* together.[133] In April 1761 the *Critical Review* blamed the unnatural public 'appetite' for more volumes of this undeservedly successful work, which inevitably 'ended in *nausea* and *indigestion*'.[134]

Tedium and the censorship-worthy coloured reviews of volumes 5 and 6 of *Tristram Shandy* in 1762. For John Langhorne, writing anonymously in the *Monthly Review*, the work's 'moral tendency' is derailed by 'libidinous ideas and indecent allusions', 'stars and dashes', which are especially inappropriate given the author's known profession.[135] But new qualities increasingly attracted admiration, especially Sterne's augmented emphasis on sensibility: the Le Fever episode in volume 5, which showcases Toby's sentimental qualities, was widely admired, as exemplified by lengthy extracts reproduced in reviews. Sterne's talent lies 'not so much in the humorous as in the pathetic', the *Monthly Review* writes, and should be encouraged.[136] For the *Critical Review*, the Le Fever episode is 'beautifully pathetic', as Toby displays the 'warmth of a heart truly sentimental', although Sterne's inimitability here counts against him: 'these volumes can be the production of no other than the original author of Tristram Shandy' – 'the same unconnected rhapsody, the same rambling digression'.[137] The diagrammatic 'narrative lines' closing volume 6 are not mentioned in these reviews; indeed, besides typographical elements (asterisks, blanks, and dashes), Sterne's graphic experiments (including the black or marbled leaves) rarely receive comment from his early critics, although they attract much attention now.

Volumes 7 and 8 were published in 1765. Satirical parody continued to offer one way of critically engaging with Sterne's perplexing humour even while his sensibility was admired. The *Monthly Review*'s account in February mimics Tristram's fragmented syntax in evoking sea-sickness as he sails from Dover to Calais – 'I am sick as a horse, quoth I, already——what a brain!——upside down!——hey dey!'[138] – in a hectic mock-dialogue with the author:

> HOLLO! Mr. Shandy! Won't you stay and take company? you are for Calais, are you not?
>
> SHANDY. Who the D— are you? What! my old friend the Reviewer! But you see I am in a d—— hurry: ... *Plash! Dash!——Helter skelter! Neck or nothing.*[139]

---

[133] *Scots Magazine*, 23 (March 1761), 141–7.
[134] *Critical Review*, 11 (April 1761), 316.
[135] *Monthly Review*, 26 (January 1762), 31–2.
[136] *Monthly Review*, 26 (January 1762), 41.
[137] *Critical Review*, 13 (January 1762), 66, 69.
[138] Sterne, *Tristram Shandy*, vol. 2, p. 578.
[139] *Monthly Review*, 42 (February 1765), 120.

The *Critical Review* uses similar methods to more negative ends. Volume 7 is 'an unconnected, unmeaning, account of our author's journey to France', it declares, before imitating Sterne's apparently nonsensical bawdry: '—Well, says my uncle Toby, Corporal, did you see that same cock—Cock, cock, said my father—what cock?—Here my mother took a large pinch of snuff—'.[140]

Two more volumes of sermons in January 1766 helped to bolster Sterne's image as a writer capable of moralistic sentimentalism; although for the *Critical Review*, disapprovingly, 'The author of *Tristram Shandy* is discernible in every page', he 'endeavours' to 'improve' as well as to 'entertain'.[141] Shandean parody nevertheless still attracted others. A spurious 'volume IX' briefly masqueraded as genuine in newspaper advertisements,[142] but was denounced by the *Public Advertiser* on 24 February as 'NOT by the Writer of Eight Volumes' of the real *Tristram Shandy*.[143] The *Critical Review* states that 'We learn from the news-papers, that this is not the production of the Rev. Mr. S——:', drawing attention to the dialogue between different types of press title. However, the reviewer is ambivalent about Sterne's supposed uniqueness: 'we may venture to assert, that the author [of "volume IX"] has deprived that gentleman of the epithet of *inimitable*'.[144] The *Monthly Review* is more loyal to the rhetoric of inimatability: 'Not *genuine*: but not so ill counterfeited, as were some of the former imitations of Mr. Sterne's truly original manner'.[145]

By the time Sterne's genuine volume 9 appeared in 1767 it brought disappointment as well as some pleasure. For the *Monthly Review*, the novelty of Sterne's 'frolicksome' narrative method had worn off, and his 'OBSCENITY' incurs censure – 'away with your sausages,—away with your stories of a cock and a bull' – not least because it tarnishes the exquisite 'SENSIBILITY' found in the Maria episode, which the *Monthly Review* reprints almost entire.[146] The *Critical Review*, meanwhile, elaborates a whimsically imaginary scene inspired by the graphic squiggle representing 'the very flourish' of Trim's 'cudgel' in the air, illustrating celibacy: '. . . the corporal began to exercise his stick, which in one of his chie[f] manœuvres came so near Dr. Slop's nose, that my father smiled, my mother chuckled, uncle Toby frowned, and the doctor ducked his head.——'[147] The review, which includes lengthy excerpts, concludes of Sterne that 'None but myself can be my parallel'. His apparent inimitability, while sometimes

---

[140] *Critical Review*, 19 (January 1765), 65.
[141] *Critical Review*, 21 (January 1766), 49; *Critical Review*, 21 (February 1766), [99].
[142] Bandry-Scubbi, 'Les faux volumes', 34–5.
[143] *Public Advertiser*, 9771, 24 February 1766, 3; also *London Chronicle*, 1434, 25–27 February 1766, 7.
[144] *Critical Review*, 21 (February 1766), 141.   [145] *Monthly Review*, 34 (February 1766), 168.
[146] *Monthly Review*, 36 (February 1767), 98.   [147] *Critical Review*, 23 (February 1767), 135–6.

debatable, remained a consistent thread in subsequent reviews of and creative responses to his publications after *Tristram Shandy*'s last volume appeared.

A Sentimental Journey and Sterne's Correspondence

Sterne's critics and adapters were confronted with a considerable amount of mixed material in a fairly short space of time. The Sterne enjoyed in 1760 was different from that of 1767; the new publications seemingly allied under the brand label increasingly comprised disparate qualities, Sterne's supposedly indecent humour jostling alongside his pathetic, and moral, sentimentalism. The dialogue between Sterne, his critics, and his imitators that propelled the evolution of his creative output during his lifetime continued after his death in 1768, and with the reception of posthumous works.

Given the marked appreciation of pathos among Sterne's reviewers it is not surprising that he developed these qualities in *A Sentimental Journey* to general applause, but its reviews are inevitably entwined with the critical reception of Sterne's earlier publications, and with perceptions of the author himself (as cleric, as celebrity). In the first instalment in March 1768 of the *Monthly Review*'s highly favourable, two-part account, Griffiths exercises the reviewers' habit of asserting their role in Sterne's reception history: 'Now, Reader, did we not tell thee, in a former Review, (somewhat less than half a century ago) that the highest excellence of this genuine, this legitimate son of humour, lies not in his humorous but in his pathetic vein?'.[148] The review was abruptly interrupted by Sterne's death: '☞ *Poor* YORICK *was living*, when this article was sent to the press'. Accordingly, in April 1768, the review's second part opens with a eulogy that recalls *Tristram Shandy*: 'ALAS poor Yorick!'[149] *A Sentimental Journey*'s 'delicacy of feeling', 'tenderness of sentiment', and 'simplicity of expression' are praised, even if its notoriously ambiguous 'END' suggests '*somewhat* bordering rather on sensuality than sentiment'. Critique nonetheless subsides in an effusive encomium on 'the inimitable LAURENCE STERNE;—to whom we must now bid eternal adieu!—'.

These views were widely shared. The *London Magazine* translated a notice found in the *Bibliothèque des sciences et des beaux arts* – a reminder of the international network of news-sharing across geographical borders[150] – stating that 'It is well known that Mr. Yorick is the Doctor Sterne already celebrated as well on account of his sermons, as for the life of Tristram Shandy', and identifying *A Sentimental Journey* as a 'work of sentiment' with 'the power of moving

---

[148] *Monthly Review*, 38 (March 1768), 185.
[149] *Monthly Review*, 38 (April 1768), 309, 311, 318–19.   [150] Black, *English Press*, pp. 87–8.

and affecting the soul'.[151] The *Political Register* declares that *A Sentimental Journey* combines 'that original vein of humour which was so natural to [Sterne]' with 'the moral and the pathetic', leaving readers both 'instructed' and 'touched with the strongest sensations of pity and tenderness'.[152] The Shandean strain did not disappear, but it became absorbed within a more complex, and not always coherent appreciation of Sterne's heterogeneity. Indeed, the *Political Register*'s review follows with a note on John Hall-Stevenson's *A Sentimental Dialogue between Two Souls, in the Palpable Bodies of an English Lady of Quality, and an Irish Gentleman*, which is 'pretty well seasoned with the double entendre', enhancing its appeal 'to the admirers and readers of Tristram Shandy, being entirely in the stile and manner of that celebrated work'.[153]

Sterne became a standard against which to judge new publications, especially those that approximated his 'stile and manner'. However, this was not without complications, not least because Sterne's status was continually fluctuating. Samuel Paterson's journey narrative *Another Traveller!* is emblematic of competing claims to Sterne's centrality, as Paul Goring has demonstrated.[154] When first assessed by the *Monthly Review* in December 1768 it was identified as a Sternean imitation, if a good one.[155] Paterson had managed to capture the 'manner and spirit' of Sterne's style, but 'we do not think the present traveller equal to Yorick'. This fired Paterson's angry riposte, made in a now lost pamphlet, that he had not even read *A Sentimental Journey* before writing *Another Traveller!* The *Monthly Review* reprinted an excerpt from this pamphlet, accusing Paterson of 'vanity, or the lust of praise'.[156] Self-declared adaptations of *A Sentimental Journey* were even less warmly viewed than Paterson's purported imitation. According to the *Monthly Review* in May 1769, a two-volume continuation by 'Eugenius' is 'like the Sentimental Journey of Yorick' but decidedly inferior, as 'There is nothing to touch the heart, or delight the imagination'.[157] For the *Gentleman's Magazine*, it is 'without wit, humour or pathos'.[158]

Sterne's posthumous appreciation was entangled with the ongoing difficulty of mediating between different strands in his writing, both as it was retrospectively critiqued, and because new imitations challenged reviewers with how to compare them with Sterne as his authorial identity continually took shape. Many contemporary readers sought a simpler definition of what 'Sterne' comprised. Reviews and Sterneana alike significantly aided that process, and helped to disseminate a part-fictive public image. But so, too, did more Sternean material. Although, as the *Monthly Review* had it, the 'hiatus' in Sterne's life

---

[151] *London Magazine*, 38 (January 1769), 27–8. [152] *Political Register*, 2.14 (May 1768), 383.
[153] *Political Register*, 2.14 (May 1768), 383. [154] Goring, 'Authorial Authority', 185–93.
[155] *Monthly Review*, 39 (December 1768), 434–8. [156] Goring, 'Notes', 273–4.
[157] *Monthly Review*, 40 (May 1769), 428. [158] *Gentleman's Magazine*, 39 (August 1769), 398.

ruptured his ability to produce more work – 'We do not hear that he has left any materials behind him for posthumous publication'[159] – the appearance of previously unpublished works, combined with new waves of imitative pieces, contributed to the ongoing mixture of real and fake 'Sterne'.

Three more volumes of sermons, published in June 1769, were considered less worthy than Sterne's earlier sermons by the *Town and Country Magazine*, one of the two most successful magazines after 1770, and which sustained a reading network between London, other major cities, and provincial locations;[160] although 'trifling and superficial', they nevertheless demonstrate his stylistic 'ease and sprightliness'.[161] *A Political Romance* was also published in 1769, albeit in incomplete form – John Murdoch, the bookseller, claimed to have recovered it from 'oblivion'.[162] It entered the game of uncertain attribution; for the *Monthly Review*,

> This is advertised as the genuine production of that exquisite pen to which the world is obliged for The Life of Tristram Shandy, and The Sentimental Journey; but no Editor appears, to answer for its authenticity. There seems, nevertheless, to be no great reason for suspecting it to be of spurious birth;— but be that as it may, the piece is a trifle.[163]

The review also reprints an excerpt from the pamphlet's preface describing *A Political Romance*'s origin – which was copied from Eugenius's spurious continuation of *A Sentimental Journey*; Sterneana, once again, was inextricably mixed up with Sterne's authorial identity and corpus. Melvyn New and W. B. Gerard, indeed, blame both Eugenius and Murdoch for perpetuating the idea that the pamphlet's 'cumbersome title' – 'The history of a good warm watch-coat' – was Sterne's own choice.[164] It persisted, including in William Strahan's *Works of Laurence Sterne* in 1780. The first collected works in 1769, meanwhile, included Eugenius's continuation, while *Works* published in London and in Dublin in 1775 incorporated *The Koran*, that is, *The Posthumous Works of a Late Celebrated Genius*, published anonymously in 1770 by Richard Griffith. This Sternean imitation, which for Shaun Regan mixes 'plausible fiction with literary invention',[165] was so convincing for some they took it to be authentic, although for one reviewer it is 'manifestly spurious, a fraudulent imposition upon the Public';[166] for another, this is 'An

---

[159] *Monthly Review*, 38 (April 1768), 318.   [160] Mitchell, 'The Tête-À-Têtes', 16.
[161] *Town and Country Magazine*, 1 (1769), 381.
[162] Sterne, *Political Romance*, p. iv; Sterne, *Miscellaneous Writings*, p. 92.
[163] *Monthly Review*, 41 (December 1769), 485–6.
[164] Sterne, *Miscellaneous Writings*, pp. 92–3.
[165] Regan, 'The Posthumous Works'; also Regan, 'Locating Richard Griffith', 95–6.
[166] *Monthly Review*, 42 (May 1770), 360.

infamous attempt to palm the united effusions of dullness and indecency upon the world, as the genuine productions of the late Mr. Sterne'.[167]

The emergence of more 'Sterne' soon added to the mix. *Letters from Yorick to Eliza*, first published in 1773 and again in 1775, contains ten letters Sterne had written to the much younger, and married, Eliza Draper. The history of Sterne's published correspondence is riddled with editorial interventions, spuriousness, and commercial opportunism. Gabriella Hartvig has demonstrated how advertisements and contemporary reviews played a continually evolving part in complicating the picture of what was real and what was fake.[168] The *London Magazine* tentatively speculated in April 1775 that *Letters from Yorick to Eliza* 'appear to be genuine productions of Mr. Sterne', and frames the relationship as one of intimate – but chaste – affection: 'the closest union that purity could possibly admit of'.[169] Yet myth and reality, and questionable authenticity, were intertwined in this public image. When the *London Magazine* reviewed a later edition in September 1775, potential fakery ran high in the reviewer's mind: 'These letters appear to be really Sterne's', the review begins, cautiously.[170] Excerpts confirm the combination of 'poignant wit, natural vivacity, and sentimental tenderness [that] characterise the author of Tristram'. The *London Magazine*, however, was right to be suspicious: *Sterne's Letters to His Friends on Various Occasions* was the part-spurious concoction of William Combe.[171]

Lydia Medalle's three-volume *Letters of the Late Rev. Mr. Laurence Sterne, to his Most Intimate Friends* was designed as a backlash, putting her father's genuine correspondence into readers' hands.[172] The *Monthly Review* confirms the volumes' authenticity in October 1775, 'on the credit of the lady who tenders her name to the Public, as their editor', which is further secured by the inclusion of Sterne's autobiographical 'Memoirs'.[173] The review's conclusion in November 1775 firmly announces that the letters 'are genuine, and will serve to assist us in forming a more competent idea of the character of the celebrated Yorick'.[174] The *Critical Review* recognises that these letters 'are admirably expressive of the author's particular cast of genius'.[175] The *London Magazine*'s review in December 1775 rectifies its earlier mistake about the Combe volume: 'The letters are *genuine*, and in publishing them the fair editor

---

[167] *London Magazine*, 39 (June 1770), 319.
[168] Hartvig, 'Advertising Sterne's Letters', 63–86.
[169] *London Magazine*, 44 (April 1775), 200–201.
[170] *London Magazine*, 44 (September 1775), 480–1.
[171] Voogd, 'Sterne's Letters'; Howes, *Yorick and the Critics*, pp. 50–1.
[172] Sterne, *Letters: Part 1*, pp. xlviii–l.   [173] *Monthly Review*, 53 (October 1775), 340.
[174] *Monthly Review*, 53 (November 1775), 403–4.
[175] *Critical Review*, 40 (November 1775), 387.

says she complies with her mother's request', exemplified by (this time) genuine Sternean excerpts.[176] The family link – visually embodied in a frontispiece depicting Lydia with a bust of her father – seemed to confirm legitimacy. The *Gazetteer and New Daily Advertiser* printed an advertisement for Lydia's edition on 5 January 1776 that briefly quoted the *Monthly Review*'s verdict that these 'genuine' letters capture Sterne's/Yorick's 'character', a condensed form of excerpt culture that exemplifies inter-borrowing between press titles.[177] These underlining issues of authenticity, and the oscillating facets of public perceptions of Sterne's authorial image as a quixotic mixture, persisted into the next century as the living author receded into the myth-making strategies of posterity.

Later Criticism

Many of the examples discussed so far inevitably cluster around the immediate appearance of Sterne's works. However, his reception increasingly involved a retrospective summation that identified him as a significant author. Even in the early 1760s the idea that Sterne possessed a distinctive, 'inimitable' style infused contemporary reviews and Sterneana alike; it became a recurrent refrain in later decades as Sterne's reputation as an author who deserved both serious critical attention and enduring popularity increasingly took hold, in parallel with an evolving critical discourse in which significant authors – notably, novelists – were considered emblematic of modern British literature.[178] The press continued to exercise its capacity as a platform for critical commentary and for creative experimentation, and for directing authorial reputations – Sterne's included – towards 'classic' status.

Sterne was increasingly taken seriously as a subject of literary criticism. John Ferriar's assessment of Sterne's sources first appeared in *Memoirs of the Manchester Literary and Philosophical Society* in 1793, the annual publication of the Manchester Literary and Philosophical Society, one of Britain's oldest learned societies, founded in 1783.[179] It was reprinted in the *Annual Register* for 1793, and later expanded in book-form as *Illustrations of Sterne* (1798).[180] Ferriar reveals Sterne's extensive and sometimes unacknowledged borrowings from other writers, but also emphasises the skill needed to weave such a complex network of sources, which stamps Sterne's genius: he deserves sustained critical attention as a 'satirical and ethical writer of note'.[181]

---

[176] *London Magazine*, 44 (December 1775), 649–50.
[177] *Gazetteer and New Daily Advertiser* 14,623, 5 January 1776, 1.
[178] Raven, *Business of Books*, pp. 224–5.
[179] Ferriar, 'Comments', pp. 45–86; Howes, *Yorick and the Critics*, pp. 81–3.
[180] *Annual Register* (1793), 379–98.   [181] Ferriar, 'Comments', p. 45.

Ferriar's claims about Sterne's 'plagiarisms' re-emerge in George Gregory's *Letters on Literature, Taste, and Composition* (1808), but fuel his critique of Sterne's 'unclassical' method of writing: 'all regard to connexion and arrangement [is] thrown aside'. The *Monthly Review*, assessing Gregory's work in 1810, protests: 'the arrangement and connection of sentences' in Sterne's prose is 'harmonious' and 'He balances words to a fault', while his 'feeling and humour' are incontestable, especially in Le Fever's tale and Uncle Toby's character.[182] The appraisal of Sterne's style positions him as worthy of serious literary criticism at a point when his classic status was becoming increasingly established.

Critical discussions were far from universally favourable, though; nor did they promote Sterne as an unproblematic author. Changing tastes played their role in shifting appreciations; a backlash against sensibility motivated one critical essay printed in March 1791 in *Walker's Hibernian Magazine* – published in Dublin from 1771 to 1812, and adding a thread to the cross-weave of Anglo-Irish book and news trades. It accuses Sterne of having 'poisoned his age and country with the most universal affectation', encouraging doppelganger 'forlorn Marias breathing their sympathetic sorrows at a ball', referring to Maria's popularity as a masquerade character, 'and holy brahmins heightening the stolen enjoyments of adultery with scraps and sentiments of morality', a nod towards Sterne's sign-off ('Thy BRAMIN') in *Letters from Yorick to Eliza*.[183] The critic parodies the most objectionable features of 'Sternean' sentimental writing to secure his point. For one contributor to the *Lady's Monthly Museum* in September 1813, however, pathetic scenes, especially those popularised by reprinted excerpts and anthologies – Le Fever, Maria, *A Sentimental Journey*'s dead ass at Nampont – inspire 'uncommon pleasure', while Sterne's sermons 'abound with pathos and originality'.[184] An essay comparing Henry Mackenzie and Sterne in the *New Monthly Magazine* in 1820, meanwhile, concludes that while Sterne 'has deeper touches of humanity' he is too erratic and unpredictable to stir consistent emotions: 'He sweeps "that curious instrument, the human heart," with hurried fingers, calling forth in rapid succession its deepest and its liveliest tones, and making only marvellous discord'.[185]

Where to place Sterne and what to make of his contribution as a writer remained continually contested. In the early decades of the nineteenth century, essays such as these participated in an increasingly developed literary-critical discipline, partly shaped by reviewing cultures, which assessed authors living

---

[182] *Monthly Review*, 61 (March 1810), 256; the Gregory quotation is cited in this review.
[183] *Walker's Hibernian Magazine* (March 1791), 242.
[184] *Lady's Monthly Museum*, 15 (September 1813), 134–7.
[185] *New Monthly Magazine*, 13.74 (March 1820), 324–5.

and dead to forge the notion of a national literature. Sterne remained a persistent thread, problematic and yet integral to that history.

3 Excerpt Culture

Eighteenth-century reading habits involved 'sampling, excerpting, and revisiting' books rather than reading them whole, Abigail Williams suggests.[186] The press amply catered for such practices with an abundance of short pieces suited to time-bound opportunities for reading, alone or in company. Most early reviews of Sterne reproduced passages from his texts, effectively making his writing available to readers as a fragmented compilation of excerpts; sometimes, reviews of Sterneana also included extracts, bringing critical and creative responses into dialogue with each other. Newspaper advertisements, too, occasionally included short quotations from the work for sale, and even from its reviews; for instance, the *Gazetteer and New Daily Advertiser*'s notice for Lydia Medalle's *Letters* reprinted an excerpt from the *Monthly Review*'s account.[187] This complemented the proliferation of excerpts reprinted as standalone items. Accounts of Sterne's reception often overlook this important feature of how, by being dispersed through excerption, his works reached the widespread audiences catered for by diverse press publications.

Sternean Excerpts, in Reviews and Freestanding

Printing lengthy excerpts from the work discussed within a review – as was often the case for Sterne's publications, as we have seen – brought texts into a greater arena of accessibility than might otherwise have been available to many readers, had they solely had recourse to books; but readers' perception of the work was also influenced by the editorial intervention excerption inevitably involves, and by the framework of commentary and interpretation in which an extract was typically placed. One of the short announcements of *Tristram Shandy*'s volumes 3 and 4 printed in the *London Magazine* in February 1761, for instance, offers a few words of analysis: this is a 'whimsical, amusing piece, which is wonderfully digressive'. Because Sterne 'has been pretty severely lash'd by the Criticks and the graver sort of Readers', this review reprints choice morsels to prove them wrong.[188] The excerpted passages are spliced together, with no distinguishing divisions besides quotation marks, serving as a miniature, condensed anthology.

Indeed, by recirculating these excerpts, the press acted as an antecedent to, and later ran parallel with, popular anthologies of extracts, a comparison

---

[186] Williams, *Social Life*, p. 74.
[187] *Gazetteer and New Daily Advertiser*, 14,623, 5 January 1776, 1.
[188] *London Magazine*, 30 (February 1761), 100–102.

compounded by the publication of magazine annuals, such as the *Annual Register*, *The Beauties of all the Magazines Selected* (1762–64), and *The Manchester and Liverpool Museum: or, the Beauties of All Magazines Selected* (1779). George Kearsley's series of book anthologies first published *The Beauties of Sterne* in 1782, which had run to thirteen editions by 1799.[189] It selected passages that emphasised Sterne's moralistic pathos, but increasingly included more humorous excerpts (although minimising bawdry) to give a fuller picture of the author's increasingly recognisable style as critical opinion seemed to consolidate what it comprised, and how far it qualified Sterne for classic status. Anthologisation nevertheless involved the selection, pruning, and curation of the chosen excerpts in line with an editorial agenda that determined which image of Sterne would thereby be promoted.[190] Press titles that reprinted Sternean extracts exerted a comparable editorial management of Sterne's text in what they selected and what they excised, and how those excerpts were framed. The *Monthly Review*'s favourable account of the Maria episode in volume 9, for instance, is exemplified with a long quotation; however, it excludes the 'ill-timed stroke of levity' that closes the episode in *Tristram Shandy*: '——What an excellent inn at Moulins!'[191] Sterne's flourish threatens to '*spoil all*', 'like a ludicrous epilogue, or ridiculous farce, unnaturally tagged to the end of a deep tragedy'.[192] By omitting it the reviewer anticipates Sterne's anthologists, who also deleted this closing quip on similar grounds in the ongoing process of crafting his public image for new critical and commercial agendas.[193]

The recirculation of Sterne's texts through reviews and advertisements paralleled the extensive dispersal in the press of excerpts from his works as standalone items. Nicholas Seager describes how, in the earlier eighteenth century, the 'practice of reprinting fiction in newspapers reflected and enhanced the novel's appeal, as newspapers helped to widen and democratize the readership for fiction'.[194] By the century's later decades this had become more ad hoc – and potentially even more democratising. As early as January 1760 the *Gentleman's Magazine* reproduced the portrait of Yorick from *Tristram Shandy*'s first instalment,[195] which reappeared in the *London Chronicle* and in the *Royal Female Magazine* in February, the latter with a cautionary headnote about the 'wantonness' of Sterne's 'wit'.[196] The *Annual Register* for 1760 likewise illustrates its review of 'this book so universally read' with the

---

[189] Newbould, 'Wit and Humour', pp. 143–8. [190] Cook, 'Authors Unformed', 290.
[191] Sterne, *Tristram Shandy*, vol. 2, p. 784. [192] *Monthly Review*, 36 (February 1767), 99.
[193] Howes, *Yorick and the Critics*, pp. 64–5. [194] Seager, 'The Novel's Afterlife', p. 112.
[195] *Gentleman's Magazine*, 30 (January 1760), 35–7. Cash, *Later Years*, p. 21; Bandry-Scubbi, 'Sterne recyclé', 15.
[196] *London Chronicle*, 2–5 February 1760, 124–5; *Royal Female Magazine* (February 1760), 56–60.

excerpted Yorick portrait, as does a 'Sentimental Biography' of Sterne/Yorick printed in the *Sentimental Magazine* in 1774.[197] The Le Fever episode – which Sterne part-serialises in *Tristram Shandy* as a fragmented story '*continued*' across several chapters, seemingly parodying contemporary serialisation practices harboured by the press – was extensively excerpted. The *Gentleman's Magazine* reprinted it in January 1762, but '*omitted several little circumstances to reduce it to a moderate length*'; nevertheless, this is '*a master-piece in its kind, and does the Writer great credit*'.[198] A biography of Sterne in the *Sentimental Magazine* of January 1774 repeats the 'masterly' accolade in commending the excerpted story's pathos, which 'would have made its author immortal, though he had never written anything else'.[199] Almost as soon as volume 9 of *Tristram Shandy* appeared, Maria's story was reprinted in the *London Magazine* in February 1767 to comparable acclaim.[200] Arguably, without Yorick's portrait, the Le Fever episode, and Maria, *Tristram Shandy*'s critical and popular endurance would have been less secure, as their moralistic sentiment redeemed its perceived indecency; in fact, they played a vital role in establishing Sterne's critical and popular legacies. Reprinted extracts from his sermons around this time similarly helped to confirm his standing as a moralist; the *Scots Magazine*, for instance, reproduced an excerpt of 'The History of Jacob, considered' in March 1766, with a brief headnote.[201]

The culture of excerption in the press nevertheless complicated the nature of the 'Sternean' publications made available. Extracts from Sterne's memoirs and letters, for one, were riddled with prevailing authenticity/fakery issues, not least because press publications in this period 'normalized' reprinted correspondence 'to fit [their] own house style'[202] – and because they reprinted fabricated Sternean items. The web of materials borrowed between titles assisted the dispersal of doubtful matter across a geographical spread. In January 1771 a letter apparently by Sterne was reprinted in the *Scots Magazine*, and then in February in the *Hibernian Magazine*, the *General Evening Post*, and *The Craftsman; Or, Say's Weekly Journal*; it subsequently reappeared in the *London Magazine* in March 1774 and in the *Weekly Miscellany* in April.[203] Although shared across multiple press titles, this was actually a fake letter that

---

[197] *Annual Register* (1760), 247–9; *Sentimental Magazine*, 2 (January 1774), 4–7.
[198] *Gentleman's Magazine*, 32 (January 1762), 32; see also *London Magazine*, 31 (January 1762), 16–21.
[199] *Sentimental Magazine*, 2 (January 1774), 4–7.
[200] *London Magazine*, 36 (February 1767), 78–9.   [201] *Scots Magazine*, 28 (March 1766), 142.
[202] Sterne, *Letters: Part 1*, p. 124.
[203] *Scots Magazine*, 33 (January 1771), 33; *Hibernian Magazine*, 1 (February 1771), 8; *General Evening Post*, 5825, 9–12 February 1771, 2; *Craftsman*, 656, 16 February 1771, 2; *London Magazine*, 43 (March 1774), 136–7; *Weekly Miscellany*, 11 April 1774, 38–9.

would appear in Combe's *Sterne's Letters to His Friends on Various Occasions* in 1775.[204] This volume also included versions of Sterne's letters to Garrick, which, as Peter de Voogd explains, had previously appeared in the *Public Advertiser* in 1770.[205] The *London Chronicle* printed a selection of Combe's forgeries in June 1775 with an explanatory note suggesting the 'editor' anticipated acquiring more.[206] The *Chester Chronicle* reproduced the same letters in July 1775, with a modified explanation (ironically) praising the 'inimitable author'.[207] The *London Chronicle* and *Public Advertiser* carried sham Sterne letters in 1787, which were published the subsequent year in Combe's third spurious collection, *Original Letters of the Late Reverend Mr. Laurence Sterne, Never Before Published*, the title echoing the phrase sometimes repeated alongside newspaper excerpts (not always truthfully).[208]

Lydia's authentic *Letters of the Late Rev. Mr. Laurence Sterne* was, as we saw, intended to thwart such specious publications.[209] Her edition also provided a mine of opportunity for excavating Sternean fragments. The *Monthly Miscellany*, for instance, reproduced two letters from this edition as early as November 1775, with the promise '[*To be continued*]' – the familiar sign-off for serialised fiction that, effectively, turns Sterne's biography into a story.[210] The hitherto unseen 'Fragment in the Manner of Rabelais', also printed in Lydia's edition, appeared in the *London Magazine* in January 1776.[211] It reprints the modified version of Sterne's text found in *Letters*: the original 'I know no more of Greek & Latin than my Arse' becomes 'than my horse'. Melvyn New and W. B. Gerard observe that Lydia 'worked to exercise as many traces of Rabelaisian bawdry as possible'; this sanitised version remained the only publicly available text until 1972.[212] The magazine's editor, however, adds an envoi, responding to the fragment's promise of more 'in the very next Chapter': 'Alas! poor Yorick! thou wilt write no more chapters.'

The appearance of posthumous correspondence coincided with, and perhaps helped to fuel, interest in Sterne's biography, and the part-fictional personae with which he was associated; new biographies incorporated extracts from Sterne's writings, and even from Sterneana, and reflected the emerging critical evaluation of his work. The *Sentimental Magazine* printed at least three

---

[204] [Combe], *Sterne's Letters*, pp. 1–6.
[205] Voogd, 'Sterne's Letters'; see also Sterne, *Letters: Part 1*, p. 124.
[206] *London Chronicle*, 2895, 27–29 June 1775, 1.   [207] *Chester Chronicle*, 11, 10 July 1775, 4.
[208] *London Chronicle*, 4846, 17–20 November 1787, 5; *Public Advertiser*, 16692, 17 November 1787, 2.
[209] *London Magazine*, 43 (March 1774), 136–7.
[210] *Monthly Miscellany*, 3 (November 1775), 516–19.
[211] *London Magazine*, 45 (January 1776), 17–18.
[212] Sterne, *Miscellaneous Writings*, pp. 152–7.

different examples in two years, one of which (in November 1775) reproduced Sterne's 'Memoirs' from Lydia's edition.[213] The *Sentimental Magazine*'s 'Sentimental Biography' of 'Laurence Sterne, commonly known by the name of Yorick' of January 1774 condenses passages from John Hill's part-fictional '*Anecdotes of a Fashionable Author*' from 1760 into a compacted excerpt.[214] By 1774, of course, more was known about Sterne, and a much larger body of work was available than in 1760: his career could be retrospectively evaluated. The piece describes the social capital of Sterne's quixotic celebrity – 'It was considered as a matter of pride to have spent an evening with the author of Tristram Shandy' – but commends *A Sentimental Journey* as Sterne's greatest achievement, 'one of the most elegant and engaging compositions in any language'. Yorick is his most recognisable authorial persona, confirmed by an excerpt from the *Tristram Shandy* portrait and a eulogistic 'Epitaph' to Sterne/ Yorick first printed in *Occasional Verses on the Death of Mr. Sterne* (1768) – which were 'not destitute of merit', allowed the *Critical Review*.[215]

The well-documented letters exchanged between Sterne and Ignatius Sancho in 1762, meanwhile, fuelled a booming excerpt culture of their own.[216] Printed in Lydia's edition and in *Letters of the Late Ignatius Sancho* (1782), which lacked Sterne's reply, these letters were recirculated, usually as a pair, in numerous newspapers and magazines, both in Britain and in America.[217] London-based and provincial titles reproduced them from 1775 onwards, including the *Annual Register*, the *Monthly Miscellany*, the *Sentimental Magazine*, the *Chester Chronicle*, and, in 1792, the *New London Magazine* and the *Town and Country Magazine*.[218] The *Boston Magazine* reprinted the *Critical Review*'s brief life of Sancho and two of his letters in June 1784, noting 'his correspondence with the celebrated Sterne'.[219] The exchange reappeared in the Philadelphia-based *Evening Fire-Side* in 1805, suggesting its currency at a time of ongoing debates surrounding Abolition. Sterne's albeit unaffirmed position on slavery was doubtless consolidated by his alliance with Sancho through these widely reprinted letters, complemented by the extensive redeployment of quotations from his works to support antislavery discourse: *A Sentimental Journey*'s 'slavery ... thou art a bitter draught' became a popular catchphrase, readily disseminated by the press.[220]

---

[213] *Sentimental Magazine* (November 1775), 493–5. See also *Sentimental Magazine* (December 1776), 556.
[214] *Sentimental Magazine* (January 1774), 4–7.   [215] *Critical Review*, 25 (April 1768), 312–13.
[216] Barker-Benfield, *Ignatius Sancho*, pp. 17–72.   [217] Gerard, 'Laurence Sterne', pp. 197–8.
[218] Solomon, 'The Anti-Slavery Legacy'.   [219] *Boston Magazine*, 1 (June 1784), 328.
[220] Sterne, *A Sentimental Journey*, p. 96. Gerard, 'Laurence Sterne', pp. 190–6.

The excerpt culture of the press, then, contributed significantly towards cultivating Sternean branding. A combination of curation (editing, selectiveness) and re-contextualisation (including paratextual commentary) emphasised certain aspects of Sterne's public image, and shaped it in ways distinct from, or which imaginatively elaborated on, his actual persona or writing. Excerpts added to Sterne's ongoing visibility in the press, and so to his recognisability as an author worth noting.

Sternean Excerpts in Recitals

The newspapers regularly advertised a type of performance allied to excerpt culture that was also linked with the theatrical entertainments which were highly popular in eighteenth-century life: recitals of extracts from favourite authors. A host of venues in London (Freemasons' Hall on Great Queen Street, Coachmakers' Hall, Cheapside) and beyond the capital catered for a growing interest in oratorical readings, and for the related popularity of public debates on topics ranging from whether reformed rakes could make good husbands to Abolitionism.[221] Some programmes enhanced the entertainment by accompanying recited passages with music. Sterne features prominently on such programmes, which add an oral node to the network of recirculated Sternean materials. Advertisements for and reviews of these events helped to keep his name current, and sustained consciousness of his best-known passages and characters.

As Abigail Williams observes, this was 'the great age of elocution', and a period during which reading aloud and listening were important communal activities.[222] The fragmentary nature of Sterne's writings, or at least their suitability to excerption, made them natural choices for recitations, especially for aspiring orators who could practise their talents in delivery by reciting textual passages deemed capable of emotive stimulation or of inciting laughter. Sterne's texts appealed to both domains. Certain performers were noted for their skill in the art. The *Gazetteer and New Daily Advertiser* of 9 February 1769, for instance, prints a letter from a correspondent praising Thomas Sheridan, actor and orthoepist (and the playwright's father) for his recitation of Dryden at the King's Theatre, Haymarket: 'I was astonished at the display of the wonderful power and beauty of our English poetic numbers manifested by his delivery'.[223] Sheridan was to team up with John Henderson, a well-known actor on the London stage, for a sequence of highly successful recitations, with Sterne's

---

[221] *Gazetteer and New Daily Advertiser*, 16,585, 19 February 1782, 1; *Gazetteer and New Daily Advertiser*, 17,926, 25 May 1786, 1, 3.
[222] Williams, *Social Life*, p. 11.
[223] *Gazetteer and New Daily Advertiser*, 12,461, 9 February 1769, 4.

texts a consistent feature; Henderson was a noted Sterne enthusiast, a member of the 'Shandean society', and the author of Sterne-inspired verse.[224] The Sheridan-Henderson recitations were popular and successful for several years; they contributed significantly towards bringing Sterne to new arenas of reception.

The *Gazetteer and New Daily Advertiser*'s theatrical intelligence column of 28 February 1785 reports on 'the combined readings of these Gemini of speech-famed heroes, Sheridan and Henderson'. Henderson's performance included 'Sterne's Sentimental Journey, [and] Swift's verses on his own death', to great acclaim: 'No reading, no recitation, not excepting even Garrick in his Ode, was so neat, so entertaining, so abundantly fraught with the power of pleasing'.[225] The Sheridan-Henderson duo was again warmly commended in the same paper on 3 March.[226] Sheridan was 'sublime as usual, elevated and successful', reading from Milton and Johnson; but Henderson garners the greatest praise, especially for his 'talent for gay and humorous personification', while 'His reading of Sterne is the highest accomplishment of the art', especially from *A Sentimental Journey*: 'The *Grisette*, and the scene in the box at the Opera, with the old Officer, the pigmy, and the German giant, were executed with such lively sensibility, with so fine a delineation of the gentleness of Sterne'. Henderson was admired for his versatility and ability to move his audience: 'every bosom was affected with kindred emotions'. A review of Saturday, 5 March in the *Gazetteer* was more doubtful of Henderson's talents, at an albeit 'brilliantly attended' session: 'Mr. Henderson read the story of *Maria*, in the Sentimental Journey, with much feeling; and a portion of Tristram Shandy, where as there was more character, and less of the simply pathetic, his talents were more happily displayed than in the former'.[227] For this reviewer, Henderson excelled in 'Strong and diversified character—masculine passions', but 'It requires tones more tender and liquid than those of Mr. Henderson, for the vibrating touches in the story of Maria'. This short notice does not identify the passages from *Tristram Shandy*, but a clue comes in an advertisement printed in the *Gazetteer and New Daily Advertiser* and in the *Morning Herald* on 8 March; at Freemasons' Hall, Henderson read the Le Fever episode and 'A passage from the Sentimental Journey', while Sheridan recited '—Sterne's Sermon on the House of Feasting and the House of Mourning'.[228]

---

[224] Brewer, *Afterlife*, pp. 187–8; Newbould, *Adaptations*, pp. 25–6.
[225] *Gazetteer and New Daily Advertiser*, 17,540, 28 February 1785, 3.
[226] *Gazetteer and New Daily Advertiser*, 17,543, 3 March 1785, 3.
[227] *Gazetteer and New Daily Advertiser*, 17,544, 5 March 1785, 3.
[228] *Gazetteer and New Daily Advertiser*, 17,547, 8 March 1785, 1; *Morning Herald*, 1362, 8 March 1785, 1.

The combination of aesthetic pleasure and affective force, however, was never very far from the commercialised contexts for recirculating the Sternean brand. The world of theatrical entertainment was particularly allied to profitability driven by audience approval, of which recitals served as an extension, particularly when noted orators and celebrated actors attracted sizeable audiences. The Hereford-published *British Chronicle* reprinted a report from the London newspapers of Henderson and Sheridan's final recital at Freemasons' Hall in March 1785, which shrewdly observes the mixture of elements qualifying these recitals' success. Sheridan gave 'force and variety', and Henderson read powerfully 'from his favourite Sterne', but the review also observes that 'These readings have turned out a very profitable *badinage* to the two lecturers', which earned them about '400 l. each', 'One proof out of many, how much *novelty* is in repute'.[229] A critique reminiscent of earlier reviews of Sterne's work as attention-grabbing and money-making, the reviewer similarly directs blame towards the consumer who buoys the market for such literary commodities, whether of new publications, anthologies of excerpts, or the recital of fragments that seemed designed for shortened attention-spans among the easily satiated. The *Morning Chronicle* and *English Chronicle* simultaneously printed a less ambiguous report of this final performance of the Sheridan-Henderson pair: 'The room was quite full; and full it deserved to be'. The review praises the 'admirable contrast' between 'Prior's Epitaph on John and Joan' and 'Swift's Hamilton's Bawn', while 'The Grisette from the Sentimental Journey, and the triumph of Shandyism, and Le Fevre' were recited by Henderson.[230] Sterne's writings single-handedly offered material embodying both pathos and comic humour.

Freemasons' Hall supplied the venue for recitations by other performers, including Mr (Willoughby?) Lacy, who organised a series of apparently highly successful events that featured Sterne's texts prominently on their programmes. The *Morning Post* of 26 May 1786 congratulated Lacy on a performance attended by a 'numerous and respectable audience'; a Sternean allusion assists the compliment, as 'To pass the *Remise doors* without that peculiar tribute of applause due to his merit, would be to confess ourselves destitute of taste or judgment'.[231] 'The Remise Door' was one of Lacy's recitation passages, delivered, for instance, in January 1787, alongside 'The Monk', 'The Snuff-Box', and 'Montriul' (which chapter version is not specified) and excerpts from Goldsmith, Pope, Milton, Hester Thrale, and Gray.[232] The *Gazetteer* advertises

---

[229] *British Chronicle*, 765, 31 March 1785, 3.
[230] *Morning Chronicle*, 4953, 29 March 1785, 3; *English Chronicle*, 974, 26–29 March 1785, 3.
[231] *Morning Post, and Daily Advertiser*, 4141, 26 May 1786, 3.
[232] *Gazetteer and New Daily Advertiser*, 18,140, 30 January 1787, 1.

a similar event at this venue on 7 August 1786 that combined text and music: Lacy recited 'STERNE'S MARIA, Second Part' and an excerpt from George Keate's *Sketches from Nature* – an acknowledged Sternean imitation – while Miss (M.?) Mahon sang 'MARIA'S EVENING SERVICE to the VIRGIN', composed by Thomas Billington.[233] These readings were charged at 5s entrance, attracting a perhaps more genteel audience compared with the entry-price ranging from 6d to 3s to see horse-riding feats and musical 'IMMITATIONS [sic]' at Astley's Amphitheatre that same evening, or *The Disbanded Officer*, 'an Address, called THE NEWS-PAPER' and a musical farce at the Theatre Royal, Haymarket for entrance fees ranging from 1s to 3s 6d. Lacy nevertheless organised a subscription event at Freemasons' Hall on 16 December 1786 with an equally varied programme, as advertised in the *Morning Post*: there were readings from *Don Quixote*, Pope's *Iliad*, and Crabbe's *The Village*; pieces by Handel, Haydn, and Antonio Sacchini; and excerpts accompanied by music, including 'Maria's Evening Service to the Virgin' performed by Miss (Georgina) George.[234] According to a newspaper review of 18 December, the event 'drew a flattering assemblage' and was by far the most 'superior' of all similar previous entertainments; Georgina George 'very properly received abundant applause' for her rendition of Billington's Maria piece.[235]

The extractability of Sterne's pathetic vignettes, and their intensified sensibility, made them particularly suited to affective recitation, especially when conveyed through a powerful delivery by an admired performer.[236] After Henderson's death in 1785, a poem printed in the *New Lady's Magazine* in September 1786 commemorated 'our second Garrick', and the literary works which brought his skills to the fore:

> He, who the best explain'd his fav'rite *Sterne*,
> At *Trim* could smile, or o'er *Le Fevre* mourn;
> Walk to the bowling-green with *Uncle Toby*,
> Then mount behind him on his darling hobby—[237]

Henderson transmitted his immersive pleasure in his favourite author to the audience, who could imaginatively accompany him on these journeys into Sterne's fictional worlds. Aesthetic and commercial viability merged in this dimension of marketing, or capitalising on, the Sternean brand, combined with the appeal of celebrity actors. The success of Henderson's reading of Sternean

---

[233] *Gazetteer and New Daily Advertiser*, 17,989, 7 August 1786, 1.
[234] *Morning Post, and Daily Advertiser*, 4316, 16 December 1786, 1.
[235] *Morning Post, and Daily Advertiser*, 4317, 18 December 1786, 3.
[236] Williams, *Social Life*, pp. 215–19.   [237] *New Lady's Magazine*, 1 (September 1786), 437.

excerpts (and his Shandean club activities) was still noteworthy in 1886, featuring in Austin Brereton's biography of the actor in *The Theatre*.[238]

Brereton's piece reflects back on the popularity of a social practice that has, perhaps, now slipped from view compared with the attention that dramatic performances have received, and theatrical experiences more widely. Recitals highlight one performance-based arena for creatively reusing literary texts, such as Sterne's, bringing them into new contexts of purpose and reinterpretation. Although London was the centre for such recitals, in particular when they featured a celebrated performer such as Henderson, they were nonetheless found in other British cities and towns – and even abroad – with Sterne providing a running thread. The *Morning Chronicle* and *English Chronicle* followed their simultaneously published, favourable report on Sheridan and Henderson's final evening of recitals on 29 March 1785 with an account of copy-cat performances outside the capital. The reviewer writes that 'Mr. Pratt who is, *litterally,* [sic] pursuing the same *Course* with Messrs. Sheridan and Hendersen [sic] in town, has met equal success at Bath, where he has already recited at the New Assembly Rooms, before an elegant and brilliant auditory'.[239] Sterne is the most recited author: 'The Monk- - -The Snuff-box- - -The Starling, from Sterne', followed by 'The Sword Reclaim'd' ('The Sword. Rennes' from *A Sentimental Journey*), the Le Fever episode, and 'Maria' (which version is not identified). The other selected excerpts represent variety: Goldsmith, Gray, Collins, Pope, Milton, and some women writers – Thrale and Miss Aikin. The reviewer's observation that 'judicious *precepts*' are interspersed among the recited passages, which 'are designed to serve as examples' of the moral, suggests how (as with reprinted excerpts) the standalone extract is couched in a critical commentary that reinforces its supposed meaning to the audience, shaping their interpretation.

Recitals provided an aural equivalent to the fragmented reading experience harboured by a newspaper or magazine, and the temporal sense with which it cohered; but, like literary anthologies and the excerpts embedded in reviews, they could also be conjoined to propel a particular agenda. As with anthologies designed to mould moralistic sensibility, the excerpts selected for recitals allied oratorical skill with affective power, promoting sentimentalism's potential as a socially bonding force; this could be harnessed to project politicised agendas. Alongside popular passages reinforcing ethical sentiment, such as 'Maria' and 'The Monk', those which spoke to antislavery discourse also featured on recital programmes: 'On Liberty and Slavery, from Sterne' was recited at Coachmakers' Hall in October and December 1786,[240] for instance, and 'The Story of the Negro Girl, from Sterne'

---

[238] *Theatre*, 7 (1 June 1888), 307.   [239] *English Chronicle*, 974, 26–29 March 1785, 3.
[240] *Morning Chronicle*, 5447, 28 October 1786, 3.

at the Lecture Room, Covent Garden in January 1789.[241] Newspapers around this period also advertised public debates that bolstered the liveliness of such issues in the same columns as literary recitals, and the capacity for authors such as Sterne to speak to them in his evolving status as a reference point. A debate on 'Which has reflected more disgrace on human nature, Slavery in Foreign Countries, or the frequency of Public executions in our own?' was advertised alongside recitals from Sterne in the *Morning Herald* and the *Gazetteer and New Daily Advertiser* on 25 May 1786.[242] By 1806, when Abolitionist debates were intensifying, in Britain and North America, a Mrs Hamilton recited 'Sterne's Picture of Slavery' in New York, although for the *Thespian Mirror* her performance 'appears something like what the critics call *bathos*'.[243]

A network of contents-sharing between newspapers ensured that comparable entertainments in London, beyond the capital, and further afield came to the attention of a wide pool of readers, dispersing variable interpretations of the type of Sterne deemed suitable for different modes of performance – comic, pathetic, or both; allied to music or appropriate for oratorical delivery; adapted to agendas ranging from sentimental, to humorous, to political. Commonly shared literary capital was redistributed by the advertisements and reviews found in the press among multiple participants in interconnecting spheres of text, performance, and context, which traded on Sterne's marketable name and what it signified to enhance the appeal and purposes of these events.

4 Creative Reception

The organs of the press that circulated reviews and excerpts of Sterne and of Sterneana also provided an outlet for a vast, varied, and dispersed array of creative responses to Sterne that considerably swelled the number of more familiar pamphlets and books. They included allusions, fictional anecdotes, the afterlives of characters (from recycled names to new adventures), ephemera, fragmented imitations, comic essay series, and serialised fiction, especially journey narratives. They responded in various ways to *Tristram Shandy* and *A Sentimental Journey*, but also to Sterne's wider output, and to his celebrity authorial persona.

Allusions and Name-Tags

The consistent thread of allusions to Sterne in the press is not, of course, unique to his reception; Swift, Johnson, and Shakespeare (for example) all repeatedly

---

[241] *World*, 649, 27 January 1789, 1.
[242] *Morning Herald*, 1741, 25 May 1786, 1; *Gazetteer and New Daily Advertiser*, 17,926, 25 May 1786, 1, 3.
[243] *Thespian Mirror*, 1, 31 May 1806, 14.

appear as reference-points in such publications. In Sterne's case, allusions gyrated freely in sometimes entirely unrelated contexts, both identifiable with but detachable from their point of origin in a temporal and geographical span facilitated by the press. Some merely appropriated familiar name-tags and, through reiteration, disseminated them in a way that underscores the notion that *Tristram Shandy* was on everybody's lips in the initial craze surrounding it.[244] The disembodiment that Brewer identifies in how eighteenth-century authors' names served as mobile 'counters' signifying whatever the player wanted them to mean in the new contexts in which they were repurposed spread to Sterne's fictional creations, too.[245] Tristram Shandy and Trim both lent their names to dance settings: musical scores were reprinted in, respectively, the *London Magazine* (1761) and the *Royal Female Magazine* (1760) – a comparison-point for the Sterne-inspired titles Ignatius Sancho used for some pieces in *Cotillions, &c.* (1776), such as 'Shandy Hall' or 'Corporal Trim'.[246] The *Grand Magazine* printed instructions for a Tristram Shandy card game in June 1760 that bore little relation to Sterne's protagonist; his famous name was sufficient to enhance the novelty appeal.[247] Reusing Sternean characters in this way participated in a wider dissemination of name-tags that encompassed anything from racehorses to sailing vessels. Tristram Shandy, a racehorse painted by George Stubbs in 1760, is a well-known example – the *Manchester Mercury* notes a win on 6 May;[248] the *Dublin Mercury* advertises a race featuring a bay horse called Favourite, the progeny of Trim, in May 1770.[249] Meanwhile, ships were sometimes named after literary characters and listed in the papers; in September 1781 a 'Ship Tristram Shandy' appears, the Boaty McBoatface of its day;[250] in May 1796 the *Gazetteer and New Daily Advertiser* records the arrival at Deal from New York of a vessel styled Uncle Toby.[251]

Nevertheless, most recurrent allusions to Sterne traded less on labels detached from any meaningful relation to their point of origin than the associations those labels held – even for those who had not necessarily read the texts in which they appeared – entering discussions on topics as varied as noses, hobby-horses and eccentricity, forenames, or the stylistic features of writing. Sterne's compositional method features in *The Genius* in 1761, for instance, as a reference-point for describing oddity: the jumbled activity of 'ROUTS'

---

[244] Oates, *Shandyism*, pp. 11–12.   [245] Brewer, 'Tactility', 195–6.
[246] *London Magazine*, 30 (May 1761), 269; *Royal Female Magazine* (July 1760), 37.
[247] *Grand Magazine*, 3 (June 1760), 290–3.   [248] *Manchester Mercury*, 425, 6 May 1760, 4.
[249] *Dublin Mercury*, 550, 1–3 May 1770, 2.
[250] *London Gazette*, reported in *Morning Herald*, 283, 26 September 1781, 2.
[251] *Gazetteer and New Daily Advertiser*, 21,050, 30 May 1796, 2.

(crowded assemblies) is 'as curious as any chapter in Tristram Shandy'.[252] Sterne's digressive style also remained an allusive thread for years to come; one correspondent to the *Gentleman's Magazine* in November 1812 defends the author of a *History of Kent* by praising his concision: he does not 'make digressions like Tristram Shandy'.[253]

Tristram Shandy's seemingly erratic compositional style fed into wider criticisms of novel-reading as faddish, and potentially morally dangerous: Sterne's idiosyncrasies were synecdochic for a topsy-turvy society. In the *Universal Museum*'s 'The Author', a series comprising letters sent from supposed correspondents, 'Sine-Cure' claims in March 1762 'Strange world this, Mr. Author,—filled with contradictions and absurdities of all complexions—'; morality is out of kilter, as an allusion illustrates: a young woman is likely to be 'more attentive to *Tristram Shandy* and her *looking-glass*, than to the duty she owes to God and her parents'.[254] A letter to Mr Author from 'A CANTAB.' in June 1762, meanwhile, recalls the 'great eclat' of *Tristram Shandy*'s initial reception to reflect how wayward times breed odd tastes; as the author quotes from Sterne, '—*Degustibus non est disputandum* [*sic*]—That is, There is no disputing against hobby-horses'.[255] Shandean hobby horses ran wild among authors searching for the mot juste to summarise pecularity or oddity. '"Every man, as Sterne said, has his *hobby-horse*"', writes one contributor to the *Town and Country Magazine* in 1774;[256] a satirical fragment titled 'Bones' in the same magazine in 1788 echoes that 'Every man, as Shandy says, has his hobby-horse—it is certain, however, that all men have *bones*—'.[257]

Walter's theories about nominative determinism regularly provided an allusive signpost for signalling eccentricity; 'Shandy Senior' signs a letter on (mis) naming in the *Public Ledger* on 31 December 1761, for instance.[258] One contributor to the *St James's Magazine* in September 1762 invokes the subject to reflect on negative criticism levelled at magazine publications, suggesting 'the word MAGAZINE carries with it an unfavourable omen', equal to that which 'Shandy thought the name of Tristram had upon his son'.[259] The author of 'The Link-Boy', a serial published in the *London Magazine*, ironically contemplates his choice of title in February 1782: 'Like Tristram Shandy's father, I was sorely perplexed to fix on a name for this child of my fancy'; he fears that the series will never become famous if misnamed, just as 'When *Trismegistus* was cut down to

---

[252] *Genius*, XV (1761), 154.   [253] *Gentleman's Magazine* (November 1812), 419.
[254] *Universal Museum*, 3 (March 1762), 134–5.
[255] *Universal Museum*, 6 (June 1762), 305; cf. Sterne, *Tristram Shandy*, vol. 1, p. 12.
[256] *Town and Country Magazine*, 6 (April 1774), 208–9.
[257] *Town and Country Magazine*, 20 (January 1788), 8.
[258] *Public Ledger*, 2.617, 31 December 1761, 1.
[259] *St James's Magazine*, 1 (September 1762), 'To the Reader' [n.p.].

Tristram'.[260] Even in 1822 the *Calcutta Journal* printed a Shandean narrative featuring a hero misnamed Triptolemus, Rabelais-style, by the curate; his mother, Mrs Yellowley, was not pleased, 'but grumbling being to as little purpose as in the celebrated case of Tristram Shandy, she e'en sat down contented with the heathenish name'.[261]

The disntictiveness of Sterne's characters, humour, and written style rapidly became incorporated within the rhetorical cognomen of the 'inimitable Sterne' who, 'in emphatic and humourous prose, says, All men have their hobby-horses'.[262] The appraisal of Sterne as one-of-a-kind, a character-type mapped onto his eccentric writing, cohered with what Eleanor Drake Mitchell describes as 'the eighteenth-century liking for personal oddity'.[263] One essayist in *The Genius* in 1761 places Sterne on a check-list of well-known authors and their supposed identifying traits – 'the deformity of Scarron, the crookedness of Pope, the blindness of Milton or Homer, or even the long nose, or no nose of Tristram Shandy'[264] – but doubly distorts the allusion: not only is Sterne implicitly aligned with his fictional creation, unlike the other authors named, but his talent is perceived in terms of supposed 'deformity' – a pejorative eighteenth-century conception of uniqueness that was persistently attached to Sterne, and to his work, to serve wider satirical purposes.

Comic Fragments and Essay Series

The supposed distortions of Sterne's writing were refracted beyond allusions in more sustained parodies, which caricatured *Tristram Shandy* partly to expose Sterne's perceived irregularities (negatively or admiringly), and partly to reflect on wider reading habits and the book market in general. From shorter fragments to longer essay series, the press provided scope for satirical experimentation that imitated the Shandean style to these ends, especially in the immediate reactions to *Tristram Shandy*, but which also extended beyond its publication-span to encompass Sterne's other writings, too, and the evolving perception of his authorial identity.

The familiar theme of *Tristram Shandy*'s perversity, leading young, especially female readers astray emerges in a letter sent by 'Maria' to the *Public Ledger* in February 1761. Her 'papa' would not allow her to read 'the *Shandean Flatus*' he admired himself, but she took advantage of his sudden illness to read it:

> Sir, I do not wonder at my Father's admiration of his favourite Shandy; such a brilliancy of wit! such a redundancy of ——, of ——'s, faith I cannot tell

---

[260] *London Magazine*, 51 (February 1782), 57–8.
[261] *Calcutta Journal*, 3.115 (14 May 1822), 186.
[262] *Gazetteer and New Daily Advertiser*, 12,628, 2 September 1769, 4.
[263] Mitchell, 'Tête-À-Têtes', 16.   [264] *Genius*, II (1761), 21.

what: yes, now I have it—of stars ****, and dashes - - -, and points ... and lines ———, and blanks,²⁶⁵

Sternean bawdry, captured in a concentrated parody of *Tristram Shandy*'s typography, channels (pretended) concerns about reading's role in forming bad habits. These familiar traits continued to fuel inventiveness in comic fragments for years to come. Tristram's hypothetical, but undelivered chapters, also conceived of as 'blanks', recurrently attracted fascination. A new family member, 'OLD SLY BOOTS', declares in the *Dublin Mercury* in April 1770 that 'My cousin Tristram Shandy intended, if he had lived, to have obliged the world with a Treatise upon Kissing, in four books', a plan scuppered by 'the death of that facetious clerk'.²⁶⁶ For the author of 'The Speculations of a Connoisseur' in the *London Magazine* in 1826, he is struck by remarkable physiognomies, particularly noses: '—Sterne would have written a chapter upon it—'.²⁶⁷

While comic fragments provided one space in which to exercise Shandean jokes, the long-running trend for essay series penned by pseudonymous authors offered a particularly fruitful route for parodically developing Sterne-inspired themes. On 31 May 1760, in a series published in the *Monitor, or British Freeholder*, 'A FAIR TRADER' claimed the right to compose 'in the modern style of TRISTRAM SHANDY', and accordingly mimics its typography and randomness.²⁶⁸ A fragment of this essay reprinted in the *Manchester Mercury* on 24 June under the title 'A Digression' brought the imitation to non-London audiences.²⁶⁹ On 14 June, the Fair Trader mimics *Tristram Shandy*'s verbal inventiveness and conversational mode: when he promises a '*sketchical* history', an imaginary reader asks, 'Ha! Ha! do you borrow that word from TRISTRAM? ... —it is permitted in SHANDY to arange [*sic*] significant syllables to convey useful ideas'.²⁷⁰ Tristram's addresses to his imaginary readers, indeed, prompted imitation, especially as his 'Madam' embodied the appeal of suggestive writing to women readers supposed by some critics. In the first instalment in March 1762 of 'The Disasters of Tantarabobus', a series printed in the *Universal Museum*, the narrator rebukes his own 'Madam' for 'always wanting to come at the bottom of things, before we have duly considered the top', sparking self-reflexive reflections interrupted by Madam: '——But, Sir, what is all this to the purpose?——'.²⁷¹ Coinciding with the recent publication

---

²⁶⁵ *Public Ledger*, 2.343, 14 February 1761, 1.
²⁶⁶ *Dublin Mercury*, 537, 31 March–3 April 1770, 4.
²⁶⁷ *London Magazine*, 6.22 (October 1826), 247.
²⁶⁸ *Monitor, or British Freeholder*, 254, 31 May 1760, 1533–58.
²⁶⁹ *Manchester Mercury*, 432, 24 June 1760, 1.
²⁷⁰ *Monitor, or British Freeholder*, 256, 14 June 1760, 545–50.
²⁷¹ *Universal Museum*, 3 (March 1762), 152.

of volumes 5 and 6 of *Tristram Shandy*, the essay echoes criticisms of the 'unconnected rhapsody' and 'rambling digression' discerned by some reviewers.[272]

As Anne Bandry has shown, the *Public Ledger* is a fertile resource for such Sternean comic essay series.[273] In early 1760, it published a sequence of letters '*from* TRISTRAM SHANDY, *Gentleman*' to 'Bob Busby'.[274] The author adopts a Shandean theme – an account of his own birth – in the first instalment of 28 April. On 30 April, however, the paper prints a letter from 'EBENEZER PLAIN-CLOTH', who is outraged to find the *Public Ledger* tainted by 'this man of vanity, this public corrupter of our manners, this same *Tristram Shandy*', before identifying the Bob Busby letter as fake Sterne: it 'is not penned by the original *Tristram Shandy*' who, if short on 'morals', unlike this letter 'is not altogether deficient in wit'.[275] Although mimicking criticisms of Sterne's indecency, Plain-Cloth's facetious attack on 'this illegitimate child of *Shandy*' joins the cat-and-mouse game of (fictitious) correspondents who interact through a newspaper's pages. On 14 May the *Public Ledger* prints a second letter to Bob Busby refuting Plain-Cloth's accusation 'that I was not Tristram Shandy', and asserting that 'I tell you again, and again, that I am Tristram Shandy am Tristram Shandy'.[276] On 22 May Plain-Cloth now objects to the publication of Sterne's sermons under Yorick's 'unseemly' pseudonym.[277] The *Public Ledger* sequence combines parody of Sterne with critical responses to his style, morality, and celebrity persona to reflect on wider issues about authenticity and (in)imitability that clustered around him.

By 1770 and the publication of the essay series 'The Batchelor' by 'Jeoffrey Wagstaff' in James Hoey's *Dublin Mercury* assessments of *Tristram Shandy*'s stylistic traits were commonplace, but imitations could now make use of Sterne's larger output, too.[278] In the issue of 3–5 May one correspondent, 'FASTIDICUS', proposes Wagstaff a catalogue of books that includes 'A Sentimental Journey through Dublin', subsequently printed 12–15 May: it blends Shandean traits with references to *A Sentimental Journey*.[279] In undertaking to compile 'a Catalogue of noble authors' the author tours Dublin to seek out high-ranking candidates. On visiting one 'noble L—' he finds he is 'a-bed', so instead speaks to his wife, who 'was sitting on a sopha . . . reading Yorick's

---

[272] *Critical Review*, 13 (January 1762), 66.   [273] Bandry, '*Tristram Shandy*', 311–12.
[274] *Public Ledger*, 1.92, 28 April 1760, 1.
[275] *Public Ledger*, 1.94, 30 April 1760, 1. Cash, *Later Years*, p. 34; Bandry-Scubbi, 'The Visitor', 295–6.
[276] *Public Ledger*, 1.106, 14 May 1760, 1.   [277] *Public Ledger*, 1.113, 22 May 1760, 1.
[278] *Dublin Mercury*, 537, 31 March–3 April 1770, 1.
[279] *Dublin Mercury*, 551, 3–5 May, 1770, 1; *Dublin Mercury*, 555, 12–15 May 1770, 4.

Sentimental Journey'. A suggestive conversation about the 'tempting fruit' Adam found in Eden follows, but (as Yorick describes in 'The Pulse') they are interrupted by her husband.[280] Yorick-style, this narrator withholds a full explanation of what ensued: 'You want, reader, to know the result; you may guess if you will.'

Essay series in subsequent decades increasingly adapted their Sternean links to the new moment of their appearance, including shifted political and social contexts. The *Journal de Paris* printed an epistolary essay briefly serialised in the summer of 1811 entitled '*TRISTRAM SCRAG, vicaire de ***, dans le comté d'Oxford*', which uses its Sternean pseudonym as a mouthpiece for satirical commentary on British politics and economics, secured by allusions to both *Tristram Shandy* and *A Sentimental Journey*.[281] The Bristol-based, anti-radical *Country Constitutional Guardian; and Literary Magazine* published a Shandean sequence with similarly polemical dimensions, beginning in November 1821.[282] The magazine's editors declare they 'have an eye to the London press, and instruct our too credulous country residents "How to read the papers"'; they invite contributions 'in this satirical department' and promise prizes for the best. The first instalment of a short series presumably intended to fulfil these aims, '*The political Opinions of Mr. Tristram Shandy, his Family, and Friends*', gives Sterne's characters afterlife in a domestic setting where the newspapers themselves are pseudo-protagonists.[283] Tristram describes how 'we were arranged round the fire, discussing the contents of the newspaper which Corporal Trim had been reading', *The Times*. While Toby, and even Slop, quietly listen, Walter cannot refrain from interrupting, for 'his hobby was Politics'. Various Shandean traits (self-reflexive gestures, digressions, short chapters abruptly broken off) meld with satire of contemporary figures; the December instalment swipes at 'Lord Byron and Mr. Hobhouse' (dangerous radicals).[284] In February 1822, the final instalment, Tristram takes 'Sir' and 'Madam' to the kitchen to picture Trim, Obadiah, and Susannah seated 'round a blazing fire', discussing the news.[285] The political savviness of their social superiors in the parlour is diminishingly replicated here; Susannah's response to Trim's critique of the 'nonsense' of 'the Opposition Members', that '"I think such Members ... ought to be cut off, Mr. Trim ..."', turns the upstairs-downstairs dynamic of

---

[280] Sterne, *Sentimental Journey*, p. 72.
[281] *Journal de Paris*, 208, 28 July 1811, 4–5; 215, 4 August 1811, 5–7; 221, 10 August 1811, 2–5.
[282] *Country Constitutional Guardian*, 1 (November 1821), 1–2.
[283] *Country Constitutional Guardian*, 1 (November 1821), 18–22. See Heyd, 'News Craze', 71.
[284] *Country Constitutional Guardian*, 2 (December 1821), 89–90.
[285] *Country Constitutional Guardian*, 4 (February 1822), 245–7.

Sterne's comedy into a class-based satire which thrives off snobbish ridicule, while his characters inhabit afterlives that speak to new contexts.

Afterlives of Character

Emotional and psychological investment fuelled the enthusiasm with which many eighteenth-century readers embraced the rapidly expanding field of prose fiction. Fictive immersion, the desire to 'live with' a character, animated the 'imaginative expansion' that David Brewer identifies as propagating numerous afterlives.[286] Amid the craze initiated by Richardson's *Pamela*, for instance, one early reader claims that 'I have gone hand-in-hand ... with the pretty Heroine in all her Sufferings', while another says of 'the Characters' that 'I know, hear, see, and live among 'em All'.[287] Sterne himself played on this tendency by extending the narrative lives of his most popular characters: both Yorick and Maria are reincarnated in *A Sentimental Journey*.

Sterne's characters – and the author himself – enjoyed extensive afterlives: 'Sterne and his Friends, Uncle Toby, Corporal Trim, and the Luckless Maria' were all revivified in 'ANIMATED LECTURES' performed 'By LADIES ONLY' at John Greenwood's auction room, Haymarket, announced the *Gazetteer and New Daily Advertiser* in late 1780.[288] A network of family members emerges across the papers, authentic and invented, joining book-publication counterparts that include Sukey Shandy (Tristram's sister), Christopher Wagstaff (his grandfather), and Yorick's numerous nephews. Minor characters earned cameos: the *London Magazine*'s Link-Boy series had, by April 1782, created a pseudo-Shandean community that included Eugenius, a 'distant relation of Mr. Yorick's excellent friend' characterised by 'humour and vivacity'.[289] Tristram, Yorick, Walter, Uncle Toby, and Maria were nevertheless the most popular choices for afterlife; they made appearances that traded on the most distinctive traits assigned by critical reactions. Tristram and Samuel Richardson's Charles Grandison converse in one of 'Umbra's Dialogues' in the *London Magazine* in May 1782, Sterne's character defending his '*life and opinions*' against imputations of 'vice'.[290] Similarly, in 'A Description of the Kingdom of Love' – a lightly eroticised satire printed in the *Oxford Magazine* in July 1771 – a 'citadel and university' much like Vanity Fair 'swarms with professors': 'not a few are expert at *double entendres*, or what is called *smut* wrapped up in clean linen for the sake of *prudes*'.[291] As for the university's governance, 'The death of the late

---

[286] Brewer, *Afterlife*, p. 14, p. 26. [287] Richardson, *Pamela*, p. 7, p. 506; albeit puffing pieces.
[288] *Gazetteer and New Daily Advertiser*, 16,173, 28 November 1780, 1.
[289] *London Magazine*, 51 (April 1782), 149.   [290] *London Magazine*, 51 (May 1782), 211.
[291] *Oxford Magazine*, 7 (July 1771), 8–10.

Chancellor *Shandy* has made a vacancy'. Sterne's association with bawdry turned 'Shandy' into decodable short-hand for '*smut*'.

The multiple interpretative angles of Sterne's texts, and his many-peopled cast-list, nonetheless made other characters appealing reference-points in more laudable scenarios. Toby's afterlives symbolise a character-type: injured war veteran, sentimentalist, amiable humourist. The *Monthly Miscellany*'s essay on 'Liberality' in June 1774 cites him as an example of excessive benevolence at a time when its pitfalls were under scrutiny, as exemplified in Oliver Goldsmith's play *The Good-Natur'd Man* (1768). After briefly paraphrasing the Le Fever episode, the author concludes that 'Mr. Sterne thinks [the fault of Toby's oath] is an honest one', and 'the hasty result of a benevolent heart ... so full of honest, social sentiments, that there was no vacuity for reflection' – a touching trait that nonetheless serves as a warning against extreme generosity.[292]

Toby's warm-hearted military persona was redeployed in patriotic, sentimental, but also comic contexts. As the author of several 'Cards' – short notices conveying a question or a brief statement frequently printed in newspapers – his name acts as a key, opening up their intended theme. In the *Gazetteer and New Daily Advertiser* on 16 December 1769, for instance, 'Uncle Toby' addresses a list of questions to 'the public' concerning matters from civil order and rioting to politicians. The final question, to 'Mr. Printer', asks 'how many of our Patriots have lived and died without places and pensions for 45 years past?'[293] The issue of veteran pensions was long-standing; Toby was sometimes drafted in to assist the campaign. A briefer Card in the *Public Advertiser* on 3 December 1779 uses the military link to more scurrilous ends: 'UNCLE TOBY presents his Compliments to Mr. CHARLES TODD, begs to know how he does;— and hopes the *Wound* in his GROIN, (for which he has a *Fellow Feeling*) will make him much more *decent*, for the rest of his life'.[294] Somewhat similarly, the inadvertent innuendo of Toby's military terminology enters the delicate topic of ladies' underwear in the *Gazetteer and New Daily Advertiser* in June 1784; stays, considered 'very inconvenient', have ceded in popularity to the 'quilted boddice': 'in the language of uncle Toby, it may be said, all is made level with the *fosse*, except the *breast-works*'.[295]

The military associations and benevolent character-traits intensified in Toby and Trim's double-act proved particularly conducive to promoting patriotism at a time when Britain was engaged in near-constant hostilities, from the Seven

---

[292] *Monthly Miscellany*, 1 (June 1774), 281.
[293] *Gazetteer and New Daily Advertiser*, 12,728, 16 December 1769, 4.
[294] *Public Advertiser*, 14,088, 3 December 1779, 2.
[295] *Gazetteer and New Daily Advertiser*, 17,136, 11 June 1784, 2.

Years' War to the Napoleonic Wars;[296] Warren Oakley, for instance, points to the propagandism of the admirable veteran portrayed in Leonard MacNally's stage adaptation of *Tristram Shandy*, premiered at Covent Garden in April 1783.[297] Similarly, a review in the *Gazetteer and New Daily Advertiser* of Richard Griffith's (originally anonymous) five-act main-piece *Variety; a Comedy*, premiered at Drury Lane on 25 February 1782, notes that Major Seafort and his servant, Davy, are 'introduced in a scene which brings uncle Toby and Trim very strongly in the minds of the audience'.[298] For the *Morning Herald*, Commodore Broadside is 'borrowed' from Smollett, while Seafort takes 'his *military hobby-horse* from *Sterne*, which he strides most aukwardly'.[299] The *Monthly Review*, too, in assessing the printed play-text of *Variety* in April 1782, suggests that Seafort is only 'an humble imitation of Sterne's admirable Uncle Toby'.[300]

Toby's modesty, meanwhile, fuels critique of the theatre for a 'Warwickshire militia officer' who writes to the *Gazetteer and New Daily Advertiser* in September 1781.[301] In watching *The Agreeable Surprise*, a comic opera by John O'Keeffe (libretto) and Samuel Arnold (music) which premiered at the Little Theatre, Haymarket on 3 September, the correspondent 'leaped from surprize to *astonishment*' to 'warmest indignation' on hearing a '*vulgar, indecent pun*' on '*ars amand*', which brought 'bursts of applause'. While this might occasion a link with *Tristram Shandy*'s bawdry, here Toby supports the cause of virtue: 'It was a wise observation of my uncle Toby, that every thing which may create a laugh, is not therefore fit for the stage'. He acquires a cameo afterlife that also expands the Shandy family history, as 'he used to add, that his grandfather, who was a great courtier in the reign of Charles the Second, repeatedly observed, that *nature* had *veiled* many things, which it was equally unwise, wicked, and indecent, to attempt to uncover'. Toby's role as a mouthpiece for morality reinforces how *Tristram Shandy*'s reputation rested on more than its association with innuendo: early reviewers' appreciation of its sentimental qualities, as embodied in Toby, endured, including in such ironic scenarios.

The recycling of these Sternean name-tags in contexts both related to and loosened from their textual origin demonstrates Vareschi's notion of 'repetition and virtualization' in the fabrication and reattachment of such labels.[302] This applied to Sterne's own name, too, in the mingling of celebrity identity and

---

[296] Bosch, *Labyrinth*, pp. 146–55.   [297] Oakley, *Culture of Mimicry*, pp. 53–76.
[298] *Gazetteer and New Daily Advertiser*, 15,592, 27 February 1782, 3.
[299] *Morning Herald*, 414, 26 February 1782, 3.   [300] *Monthly Review*, 62 (April 1782), 262.
[301] *Gazetteer and New Daily Advertiser*, 16,447, 11 September 1781, 2.
[302] Vareschi, *Everywhere and Nowhere*, pp. 130–1.

pseudonymous personae that sustained his authorial brand; 'Sterne' makes anecdotal appearances to voice a Shandy-like opinion or witticism, or a Yorick-style sentiment, or to act as the epitome of companionable bonhomie – an impression gleaned from Sterne's conversational style of writing, and his likable oddity: for the *Monthly Review*, Sterne is caricatured as 'a sort of after-dinner-companion, who ... laughs when he can'.[303] This perception complemented the buoyant public taste for anecdotal histories, gossip columns, and 'secret lives', newspapers serving as 'channels of gossip and celebrification'.[304] Eagerness for tittle-tattle lay behind the popular 'Tête-à-tête' series printed in the *Town and Country Magazine*, mentioned in Richard Brinsley Sheridan's *School for Scandal* (1777) for its sensational stories. Sterne features in the 1788 portrait of David Williams, the Welsh philosopher and theologian, dubbed the 'Priest of Pleasure'. In his rise to celebrity, Williams 'was intimately acquainted with the late Mr. Sterne, author of Tristram Shandy', a fashionable figure who influenced both Williams's conduct and his writing.[305] Sterne-related anecdotes continued to thrive: in May 1798 the *Monthly Visitor*'s 'Gossipiana' feature juxtaposes Sterne's sketch about graffitiing his schoolroom ceiling as a boy, excerpted from his 'Memoirs', with vignettes picturing Milton, Johnson, and others.[306] The press fuelled a semi-fictive celebrity industry, even while such authorial names were elsewhere stamped with authoritative literary status.

A remarkable example of the plasticity of authorial afterlife comes from the well-known announcement of Sterne's death in February 1762, when he was very much alive. The *London Evening Post* and *St James's Chronicle* both reported that 'Private Letters from Paris bring an Account of the Death of the Rev. Mr. Sterne, Author of Tristram Shandy'.[307] As Catherine Tremain points out, 'death notices and obituaries ... were presented and offered as *news*';[308] in the *London Evening Post* Sterne's death is sandwiched between announcements of the newly appointed Chamberlain of the Exchequer and the drowning of several persons in the Neva, in Russia, from 'passing over the ice, before it was strong enough'. The rapid relay of information across an international network of correspondents inevitably introduced errors, and fact-checking was far from fool-proof, as Andrew Pettegree observes.[309] The *London Evening Post* quickly printed a brief retraction: 'The Report of the Death of the Rev. Mr. Sterne,

---

[303] *Monthly Review*, 61 (March 1810), 256.
[304] Heyd, 'Fifteen Lines of Fame', p. 112; also Heyd, 'News Craze', 62.
[305] *Town and Country Magazine*, 10 (December 1778), 675.
[306] *Monthly Visitor*, 4 (May 1798), 14–17.
[307] *London Evening Post*, 5344, 2–4 February 1762, 2; *St James's Chronicle*, 141, 2–4 February 1762, 4.
[308] Tremain, 'Life After Death', 180.   [309] Pettegree, *Invention*, pp. 256–7, p. 268

Author of Tristram Shandy, is not true; Letters from Paris of the 20th of last Month, mention that Gentleman to be in good Health'.[310]

Although, for Arthur Cash, 'Sterne dead was more newsworthy than Sterne alive',[311] his still-thriving celebrity status at this point created a curious interplay between the 'real' author and his 'virtualized' authorial persona as something that could be toyed with in the pages of a paper, as though a potted news story. The irony that the creator of Yorick – a fictional character whose death is memorialised in *Tristram Shandy*'s first volume – should be mixed up with falsified accounts of his own demise, only subsequently to be resurrected, was not lost on contemporary readers.[312] This perhaps fed into the frivolous handling of Sterne's actual death in some posthumous poetic tributes, as reviewed in the press. *Sentiments on the Death of the Sentimental Yorick, By one of Uncle Toby's Illegitimate Children* is deemed merely 'An attempt to be witty, in Mr. Sterne's manner, on the death of Mr. Sterne'.[313] *The Fig-leaf—Veni, vidi, vici, ivi: or, He's gone! Who? YORICK!* incurs outrage as an opportunistic attempt 'to pocket a few shillings by a *twelve-penny touch* on the death of the celebrated author'.[314] The commercial opportunism of reusing not only Sterne's texts but his name, and the authorial body it supposedly represented, thrived in such environments – as in numerous more sympathetic homages. For several years after Sterne's death in 1768, the press bore witness to poetic tributes that foregrounded the best-known aspects of his published works and the character-traits most readily associated with his celebrity persona, which reflected an increasing move towards critically assessing, and appreciating, Sterne as a national classic worthy of commemoration. Eulogies nevertheless sat among an eclectic array of poetic responses to Sterne.

Poetry

Newspapers and magazines favoured short contributions fitted to their constrained space, and to temporally bound reading experiences:[315] poetry was ideally suited. Sterne-related poems in these venues included eulogies to Sterne (especially as Yorick), sentimentalised verses – particularly tributes to Maria – and comic, satirical pieces that variously reflected on the author's character, his works, their reception, and broader book-market contexts. What type of Sterne-inspired verse appeared when and where partly depended on the chronology of his published output, but also shifting literary tastes, and on the type of

---

[310] *London Evening Post*, 5348, 11–13 February 1762, 1.   [311] Cash, *Later Years*, p. 127.
[312] Powell, *Performing Authorship*, pp. 211–12.   [313] *Monthly Review*, 38 (April 1768), 323.
[314] *Monthly Review*, 38 (April 1768), 323.   [315] Williams, *Social Life*, p. 74.

publication: proprietorship and anticipated readership inevitably determined the nature of a contribution.

Tristram Shandy-themed poems appeared in the press almost as soon as the first two volumes of Sterne's work were published. The *Gentleman's Magazine* printed 'TRISTRAM SHANDY' in May 1760, which comically touches upon the as-yet unborn Tristram ('a wond'rous spark'), male midwives, Sternean obscurity, and bawdry – reference-points include Cleland and Rochester.[316] The caricature of Sterne's titillated readership, especially young, impressionable girls, chimes with similar critique elsewhere: 'It puzzles and pleases, / With expecting, it teazes, / But they're left in the lurch by a *Shandy*'.[317] Similarly, also in May, the *Universal Magazine* printed 'A Lyric Epistle' addressed to '*the Students of Divinity in —— College*, Oxford', featuring advice from 'TRISTRAM SHANDY' on how to attain preferment in the church, but which suggests Sterne has another, more profitable 'trade' as a peddler of obscene '****'.[318] In June, the *Gentleman's Magazine*, again, printed 'A RECEIPT *for a Soup for* Tristram Shandy', which echoes recurrent comments on Sterne's compositional methods in its hodge-podge confection of ingredients: veal, sorrel, and so on – the herb an allusion to the death in 1702 of King William III, who fell from his horse, named Sorrel.[319] The historical reference hints at the poem's more chronologically proximate origin: John Gay's 1726 squib 'Receipt for Stewing Veal' was sent in a letter to Swift and subsequently reprinted in the *Weekly Journal* in 1727 (but misattributed to Swift), before being resurrected and allied with *Tristram Shandy*.[320] Newspapers recycle old materials, but modify them to gain currency amid new events and audiences.

The *Public Ledger* – which, as we saw, featured several creative reactions to Sterne in the early 1760s – published a poem by William Dodd on 4 March 1761 that echoes contemporary attacks on *Tristram Shandy*'s 'page immoral', a threat to virtue.[321] Melvyn New dismisses the piece as illustrative of 'the difference between the truly memorable and the merely collectible'; Dodd's poem nevertheless confirms the dialogue between the critical and creative dimensions of Sterne's reception, and of how the press helped to keep his name and his works current.[322] The *St James's Magazine* enacted these trends more positively with a contemporaneous spate of Sterne-themed comic poems. Digressiveness and ambiguous innuendo surface in December 1762 in 'A Familiar Letter of Rimes to a Lady'; the author tells his imaginary female addressee that, 'Like TRISTRUM [sic] SHANDY', he could write 'Sometimes obscure, and sometimes

---

[316] *Gentleman's Magazine*, 30 (May 1760), 243.   [317] Bandry-Scubbi, 'Sterne recylé', 19.
[318] *Universal Magazine* (May 1760), 265–6.   [319] *Gentleman's Magazine*, 30 (June 1760), 289.
[320] Barnett, 'Gay', 346–7; Cash, *Later Years*, p. 37.
[321] *Public Ledger*, 2,358, 4 March 1761, 1.   [322] New, 'Pots and Kettles', 41–2.

leaning / A little sideways to a meaning'.[323] In April 1763, a long satirical poem playfully swipes simultaneously at Sterne's style and at press cultures. Sternean 'digression' and 'ramb'ling' are now attributed to the *St James's Magazine*'s editor, Robert Lloyd – Sterne was a subscriber to Lloyd's *Poems* (1762) – for establishing 'A MAGAZINE, a wretched Olio', his 'handy-dandy' method paired with that of 'TRISTRAM SHANDY'.[324]

Lloyd's magazine used a cluster of Sterne-related poems in mid-1763 to target reviewing culture, which also illustrate the dialogue between contributors enacted via a magazine's pages. In May, 'Epistle to Mr. Lloyd' mocks Sterne's wit when advising aspiring poets: if the 'rhimer' lacks a 'bawdy jest', then 'Hey, Presto: —— let him try the magic spell, / Facetious STERNE: – four stars do just as well'.[325] In July, 'PHILO-SHANDY' pens a letter attacking the author of the 'Epistle' for having treated 'THE memory of TRISTRAM SHANDY ... somewhat cavalierly'; he offers 'the following Elegy, to vindicate the character, at the same time that I lament the loss of that truly respectable personage'.[326] Sterne, obviously, was not dead in 1763: Tristram's 'vital breath' had been stopped by too-harsh criticism; 'each *reviewing*, JACK-ASS bray'd', referring to Tristram's description of his reviewers as 'Jack Asses' who 'Bray bray—bray' (likewise the inspiration for '*An* EPIGRAM. *On* SHANDY *being* Bray'd *at*' in the *Universal Museum* in May 1762).[327] The 'Elegy' praises Tristram's/Sterne's combination of 'mirth' and 'the language of the heart', and particularly the Le Fever episode, while his humour likens him to Rabelais, Cervantes, Lucian, and Swift. The elegy is followed by 'The EPITAPH', which confirms that Tristram died from critical 'treatment too severe'.[328] Thomas Keymer suggests that this eulogy was motivated by the hiatus in the appearance of new volumes of *Tristram Shandy*.[329] It also chimes with the false announcement of Sterne's death briefly carried in newspapers the previous year. Reading Philo-Shandy's letter, the elegy, and the epitaph together emphasises how *Tristram Shandy*'s serialised appearance exposed it, and its author, to a continually oscillating critical reception mirrored in the back and forth of such imaginative responses.

Mock-eulogies such as these anticipated those crude '*penny touch*' funerary pieces, such as *The Fig-Leaf*, which sought to capitalise on the actual death of 'the celebrated author'. Laments for poor Yorick in *A Sentimental Journey*'s

---

[323] *St James's Magazine* (December 1762), 229. [324] *St James's Magazine* (April 1763), 116.
[325] *St James's Magazine* (May 1763), 199–200.
[326] *St James's Magazine* (July 1763), 312–16.
[327] *Universal Museum,* 5 (May 1762), 295; Sterne, *Tristram Shandy*, vol. 1, pp. 491–2.
[328] The only portion anthologised by Howes, *Critical Heritage*, p. 253.
[329] Keymer, *Sterne*, p. 140.

earliest reviews nevertheless found more serious counterparts in the numerous elegies that paid Sterne sympathetic tribute, many of which were funnelled through the press. 'On the Death of YORICK' appeared in the *London Magazine* in June 1768, praising Sterne's 'sympathising heart' and admiring characters such as *A Sentimental Journey*'s Monk, and Maria – unusually, the *Tristram Shandy* version, with 'her faithful kid' and 'olive foliage' in her hair.[330] This eulogy, comingling Sterne's character with those creations that best exemplify his qualities, was reprinted in Lydia's 1775 edition of her father's correspondence, now under the title 'In Memory of Mr. STERNE, author of THE SENTIMENTAL JOURNEY' (submerging *Tristram Shandy*).[331] The versification of 'A Character, and Eulogium of STERNE', also in Lydia's edition, was judged by the *Monthly Review* to be 'very pretty, though incorrect', but was nonetheless reprinted in its review of the *Letters* in November 1775, and subsequently in the *Monthly Miscellany* in December.[332]

A to-and-fro of eulogies appeared during these years. In March 1774, the *Hibernian Magazine* reprinted lines borrowed from the *St James's Chronicle*'s brief announcement of Sterne's death in March 1768, which jibed at Yorick's apparent lack of '*One Grain of* Wisdom'.[333] The 1774 poem 'To the Author of the above lines' rebukes this 'insult', and offers 'Tribute' to Yorick's creations (Le Fever, Toby, Trim).[334] The same issue of the *Hibernian Magazine* also includes 'An EPITAPH for the Rev. LAURENCE STERNE's Tomb-stone. By a LADY', which bids Sterne eternal rest free from his critics, and pictures mourners weeping over Yorick's tomb. These lines, reprinted in the *Annual Register* in 1795, precede another elegy: 'YORICK, farewell! peace dwell around thy stone'; now, his fictional creations (Le Fever, 'faithful Trim') provide a lasting commemoration, as they would later do in 'A character, and eulogium, of STERNE' in the *Chester Chronicle* in December 1775.[335] Quixotic associations promoted Sterne's reputation through his most admired characters.

These afterlife traces in poetic eulogies resurface in 'Yorick in the Shades; Or, the French Revolution' by the actor (Henry?) Lee, printed in the *Lady's Magazine* in January 1790; the by-then historic death of 'IMMORTAL STERNE! the matchless YORICK styl'd' intersects with new political events.[336] Sterne's works converge, as 'honest TRIM' damns both the '*Inquisition*' (following *Tristram Shandy*) and

---

[330] *London Magazine*, 37 (June 1768), 323, 332.
[331] Sterne, *Letters of the Late*, p. xi, pp. xv–xvi; Cash, *Later Years*, p. 351; Howes, *Critical Heritage*, p. 204.
[332] *Monthly Review*, 53 (November 1775), 403–13; *Monthly Miscellany*, 3 (December 1775), 561–3.
[333] *St James's Chronicle*, 1100, 17–19 March 1768, 4.
[334] *Hibernian Magazine* (March 1774), 154.
[335] *Annual Register* (1795), 227; *Chester Chronicle*, 33, 11 December 1775, 4.
[336] *Lady's Magazine* (January 1790), 45–6.

the despotic Bastille (recalling Yorick's musings on captivity).[337] '*Truth, Justice, Freedom*', three 'celestial maids', carry news of its fall to Yorick in 'th'*Etherial shades*'. He weeps with joy that '*British freedom* beams on *Gallia*'s shore' – values embodied by Toby, Trim, and Walter – and that 'Each tongue shall vindicate the *rights of man!*' The slippage between fictional characters and real-life author allows Sterne/Yorick to act as a mouthpiece for British liberty, promoting his position as a representative of national literature.

The perpetuation of admired characters' afterlives in the years leading up to Lee's poem, alongside the evolving appreciation of Sterne as a classic author, contributed to the new applicability of a Sterne-inspired creative piece in a different environment of international emergency. While Toby's afterlives as a sentimental patriot played their part in some quarters, Maria's prominence in the discourse of sensibility was equally significant in forging a laudable idea of what 'Sterne' signified, such as to make him a worthy spokesperson for British values. The press harboured voluminous Maria-related verse that repeatedly draws attention to her textual origins as Sterne's creation, while promoting her most admired qualities amid the broader trend for sentimental fiction.

The centrality of the reading process in accessing sentimental affect originates in *A Sentimental Journey*. Yorick, travelling through France, recalls 'poor Maria' as described by 'my friend, Mr. Shandy': 'The story he had told of that disorder'd maid affect'd me not a little in the reading'.[338] Such metatextual moments resurface in many of Maria's afterlives. The anonymous 'editor' of *Letters of Maria* (1790), for instance, recollects reading 'the *Sentimental Journey* of Sterne' while travelling through France, 'and being rather *ennuyé* ... I began to re-peruse [Maria's story]', which prompts him to visit her, Yorick-like, as though a tourist attraction.[339] Maria-themed verse recirculated in the press repeats these tendencies. '*On reading the chapter of* MARIA', contributed by 'CYPHER' to the *Sentimental Magazine* in 1773, addresses 'sad Maria' directly: 'shall thy tale / To each fond soul be dear'.[340] It is nevertheless Maria's story as related in Sterne's '*chapter*' that prompts a pitiful tear from the reader's 'eye', an emotive response akin to spectatorial illustrations depicting Yorick gazing upon Maria.[341] Cypher's poem reappears, lightly altered, in the *Town and Country Magazine* in 1787; '*On* READING STERNE'S MARIA' reiterates readerly immersion, and a mediating authorial presence.[342]

The textual source is even more overt in 'Paraphrase on Part of Sterne's Maria', printed in the Philadelphia-based *Evening Fire-Side, or Literary*

---

[337] Sterne, *Tristram Shandy*, vol. 1, pp. 143–4; Sterne, *Sentimental Journey*, p. 94.
[338] Sterne, *Sentimental Journey*, p. 149.   [339] Anonymous, *Letters of Maria*, p. vi.
[340] *Sentimental Magazine* (May 1773), 141.   [341] Gerard, *Visual Imagination*, pp. 153–5.
[342] *Town and Country Magazine*, 19 (December 1787), 571.

Miscellany in September 1806 – one indication of Sterne's American reception amid sentimentalism's international spread. The poem draws heavily on *A Sentimental Journey*'s pictorialism in describing Maria, 'by a poplar o'er shaded':

> Her form, in a robe of pure white was invested,
> Her hair, o'er her delicate hand, loosely flow'd,
> As upon it her craz'd head she pensively rested,
> And gaz'd on the flow'rs that around her were strew'd.[343]

Elaborating on the 'disorder' that Sterne's Yorick notices, this 'craz'd' Maria, 'Wildly warbling her tenderly querulous song', approximates her forerunner, Ophelia, through the narrator's viewpoint: 'I discern'd by her wild eye, her painful sensation'. By contrast, in 'To the Willow, in the Character of Sterne's Maria', printed in the *Gentleman's Magazine* in September 1785, Maria herself seeks sympathy for 'a wandering maid'.[344] The sonnet's allusion to Philomela suggests light classical affectation, but it also links with the preceding poem by the same hand, a Mrs Hughes: 'To a Linnet' speaks of a bird confined in a cage, recalling *A Sentimental Journey*'s captured starling, and complementing the entrapment characterising Maria's re-narrated story of abandoned romance.

Serialised 'Sentimental' Journeys

The sympathetic affect in poetic reinterpretations of Maria's character during this period is unsurprising given the wider (if by no means universal) enthusiasm for sentimental fiction, and Sterne's prominence as an admired proponent of the mode. Poetic pieces intensified the emotive force of recognisable prompts for a sensibility-infused response; short prose fragments provided another; and fragments looped together in a serialised narrative, etiolated over multiple issues of a press publication, another still, opening up access to fiction across a broader market.[345] Seager indicates that, while serialising novels in newspapers in earlier decades was common, 'rarer is continuation'; but in the later eighteenth century newspapers and magazines alike provided an attractive route for serialised fiction that often picked up predecessors' trailing threads.[346] While some Sterne-inspired serialised narratives strove for sensibility, though, many oscillated between sentimental and comic modes, suggesting the interpretative flexibility his writing invited, and which could be further developed through adaptation.

---

[343] *Evening Fire-Side*, 20 September 1806, 5; cf. Sterne, *Sentimental Journey*, p. 150.
[344] *Gentleman's Magazine*, 55.9 (September 1785), 736.
[345] Suarez, 'Business of Fiction', p. 32. [346] Seager, 'The Novel's Afterlife', p. 122.

Although prose fiction in these outlets has sometimes been treated doubtfully[347] – Robert D. Mayo disregards its 'uneven ... quality'[348] – more recent critics, such as Jenny DiPlacidi and Jennie Batchelor, have argued that magazine fiction deserves more serious attention.[349] Newspapers provided an equally inviting space for serialised fiction, albeit according to different layouts, readerships, and publication frequencies. In both cases, serialisation facilitated developing characters and storylines, including those drawing on well-known works, sometimes over several years; it fuelled fictive experimentation, often under the guise of anonymity or pseudonymity, which even allowed for multi-authored composition. Serialisation was particularly well-suited to conveying travel narratives, each instalment of which resembled the staging posts of a journey: newspapers and magazines carried numerous examples, fictionalised and real, either wholly or partly based on Sterne's fictions, whether foregrounding sentimental or comical strains, or combining both.

Several of these journey narratives seemed to self-identify as Sternean by adopting the 'sentimental journey' label, which Sterne appeared to have capitalised successfully – although 'sentimental' was already well-worn, as Lady Bradshaigh famously suggested to Samuel Richardson in 1749: 'Every thing clever and agreeable is comprehended in that word'.[350] By 1769 the *Monthly Review*, in assessing *Occasional Attempts at Sentimental Poetry*, echoed that 'The word *sentimental* is, like continental, a barbarism that has but lately disgraced our language, and it is not always easy to conceive what is meant by it', although liberally applied to 'a *Sentimental* Novel' and 'a *Sentimental* Journey'.[351] 'Sentimental journey' was to become a distinctive and long-lasting element of the Sternean brand, with new publications using a formula typically linked with Sterne's. Even as soon as 1781, the *Edinburgh Magazine* could complain that 'not a month passes wherein we are not pestered with sentimental journeys, adventures, &c. in the Shandean stile and manner'.[352]

The best-known example from the magazines is 'A Sentimental Journey. By a Lady', which appeared in the *Lady's Magazine* from its first issue in August 1770, until 1777 – the longest-running Sternean adaptation. The journey's female narrator pursues a tour around the British Isles through the widely popularised narrative vehicle of the coach journey. Batchelor describes it as

---

[347] Raven, *Judging New Wealth*, pp. 24–5, pp. 29–30.
[348] Mayo, *English Novel*, pp. 1–2, pp. 5–6.
[349] DiPlacidi, '"Full of Pretty Stories"', pp. 264–6; Batchelor, *The 'Lady's Magazine'*, 3–4; Batchelor, '"Connections"', 249.
[350] Richardson, *Correspondence*, p. 80.   [351] *Monthly Review*, 41 (November 1769), 390.
[352] *Edinburgh Magazine*, 54 (27 December 1781), 379–81.

'Part-homage to, and part-parody of, its Sternean namesake', but also as a 'picaresque serial'.[353] It is, indeed, reminiscent of Smollett, with its quirky characters and hazardous accidents, and of Henry Fielding in its journey-storytelling metaphors, but its dash-laden typography and style bring it closer to Sterne – it begins partway through a conversation, the title and episodic chapters recall *A Sentimental Journey*, and the humorous tone evokes *Tristram Shandy*, as do metatextual allusions. In the September 1770 instalment, for instance, the narrator says of her 'chaise' that '—It resembled the *desobligeant* mentioned in my uncle YORIC's [*sic*] *sentimental journal*'.[354] When she encounters a highwayman, interpreting sentimental body language, Yorick-style, nudges a joke about Shandean prolixity: 'he gave me such a look, as if translated, would dilate into more volumes than the Life and Opinions of Tristram Shandy'.[355]

Paul Goring points out that this serialised journey has been strangely neglected in discussions of Sterne's reception, while any comments are often negative.[356] It is 'the most affected, and ... the most unreadable of all contemporary works of magazine fiction', according to Mayo.[357] For Batchelor, 'by the standards of the novel – even by the standards of the Sternean novel – its plotting is tenuous'.[358] Yet self-reflexivity – clearly Sterne-inspired here – is integral to magazine fiction; indeed, 'Metafictional moments in this vein delighted readers for many years', Batchelor writes.[359] Goring suggests that 'A Sentimental Journey. By a Lady' deserves more scrupulous attention because of what it reveals about Sterne's reception via adaptation, but also about eighteenth-century magazines. Its mixed generic qualities and bifurcated connection with Sterne, from whom it became increasingly detached, were undoubtedly shaped by the seven-year lifespan enabled by serialisation; during this 'evolution' (as Goring puts it) over time, the content, tone, and perhaps authorship changed, until 'A Sentimental Journey. By a Lady' vanished.[360] It also exposes the commercial circumstances of magazine publication. It was significant in the launch of John Wheble's *Lady's Magazine* in August 1770,[361] and was 'clearly a highly valued component' of its emerging 'brand', Goring argues.[362] George Robinson and John Roberts acquired the title in early 1771, to the dissent of Wheble, who continued to publish his own rival *Lady's Magazine* – two editions ran simultaneously from April 1771 to December 1772.[363] For several issues, then, different versions of

---

[353] Batchelor, *The 'Lady's Magazine'*, p. 49.   [354] *Lady's Magazine* (September 1770), 50–1.
[355] *Lady's Magazine* (September 1770), 53.   [356] Goring, 'The Evolution', 68.
[357] Mayo, *English Novel*, p. 341.   [358] Batchelor, *The 'Lady's Magazine'*, p. 50.
[359] Batchelor, *The 'Lady's Magazine'*, p. 50.   [360] Goring, 'The Evolution', 82–3.
[361] Batchelor, *The 'Lady's Magazine'*, 50.   [362] Goring, 'The Evolution', 76.
[363] Batchelor, *The 'Lady's Magazine'*, p. 2, p. 8, pp. 46–8; Fergus, *Provincial Readers*, p. 235n5; Raven, *Business of Books*, p. 175.

'A Sentimental Journey, By a Lady' appeared concurrently in both versions of the title as part of a larger legal dispute.[364]

This litigation exposes the valuableness of serialisation, which, as James Raven argues, served as a marketing device that kept readers coming back for the next instalment.[365] It also opened up creative possibilities, especially in terms of readerly interaction: contributors joined the magazine's imaginary community by participating in its dynamic of imitation and innovation.[366] In the December 1770 issue of the *Lady's Magazine* one correspondent, 'THERON', offers '*A* HINT *to the Author of the* SENTIMENTAL JOURNEY' in the form of an additional chapter titled 'THE CHURCH-YARD'.[367] A '*Letter from the Author of the Sentimental Journey to* Theron' in January 1771 takes the theme of a dropped glove, representing the favour of Theron's offered chapter, which the author picks up amid a combat between 'Delicacy' and 'Vanity'. The column ends with the encouragement that '*Any favours from* Theron *will be agreeable*'.[368]

The malleability of the 'sentimental journey' label meant it readily attached itself to other magazine serialisations. The *New Lady's Magazine*, a competitor title to the *Lady's Magazine*, published 'A New Sentimental Journey through England. Written by a Lady' from March 1786 onwards.[369] Earlier, in March 1773, the *Sentimental Magazine* printed the first instalment of 'A Sentimental Journey through Life';[370] although the magazine's title suggests an emphasis on sentimentalism, its approach to sensibility was as mixed as its sometimes eclectic contents, and as the Shandean qualities of this journey. It, too, begins in the middle of things. The narrator pursues a trail of introspective reflections: 'But how came I into this *elbow-chair*?'[371] He revisits well-worn metaphors with an ironic claim to novelty: 'Life has been compared to several things, to a shadow, a bubble, a vapour, a stage-coach, &c. but I have not met with any one who has compared it to a journey, though the analogy is natural.' The episodic, titled chapters resemble *A Sentimental Journey*'s, but *Tristram Shandy* resonates in the narrator's descriptions of his mother's pregnancy, a male physician, and a character called Toby.[372]

---

[364] Batchelor, *The 'Lady's Magazine'*, 68–9; Goring, 'The Evolution', 65–6, 76–9.
[365] Raven, *Business of Books*, pp. 279–81.
[366] Batchelor, *The 'Lady's Magazine'*, p. 52; Batchelor, '"Connections"', 250–1.
[367] *Lady's Magazine* (December 1770), 219–20. *Google Books* version.
[368] *Lady's Magazine* (January 1771), 259.
[369] *New Lady's Magazine* (March–December 1786, supp. vol. 1). Batchelor, '"Connections"', 247; Raven, *Business of Books*, p. 274.
[370] *Sentimental Magazine* (March 1773), 3–4.   [371] *Sentimental Magazine* (March 1773), 1–10.
[372] *Sentimental Magazine* (April 1773), 53.

'A Sentimental Journey through Life' did not last long. The November 1773 instalment concludes abruptly with an editorial announcement:

※ We are sorry to inform our readers, that we are prevented from continuing the *Sentimental Journey through Life* . . . - - -The author having been accustomed to read in bed, one night fell asleep, and the candle catching the curtains, a fire consumed him and the bed, and destroyed all his manuscripts, which was the *Continuation of this Journey!!!*[373]

This excuse, along the lines of homework-eating dogs, cuts off a narrative that, perhaps, had become tedious to editors, author(s), readers, or all; at least it places a definitive end to the serial, compared with some 'to be continued' stories that never materialise. For James Chandler, this is clearly 'a derivative performance' that uses Sternean character-names and settings, and the 'language of vehicularity' common to sentimental journeys.[374] Derivativeness, however, testifies to how elements appropriated from Sterne's texts remained recognisable as 'his', but also to the repeatability necessary to the sentimental mode (serious or comic) more generally: recurrent sign-posts prompted readers how to react, but, in the context of serialised fiction, also reminded them of previous instalments and instilled anticipation of future chapters.

Newspapers exercised a similar capacity for serialised journeys, if energised by a different temporal pressure: they appeared more frequently than magazines, and instalments often emerged at erratic intervals. 'A Sentimental Journey through Life' briefly surfaced in the *Gazetteer and New Daily Advertiser* in September 1785.[375] It bears similarities to the *Sentimental Magazine*'s narrative of the same name in its episodic, humorous vignettes – 'The Charm', 'Pea-Straw' – but, despite the promise on 29 September that it was '*To be continued*', it does not appear that it was. Serialised journey narratives in other newspapers nonetheless enjoyed greater longevity, and a closer relationship with those in magazines in the competitive, commercialised contexts in which such publications operated.

Leonard MacNally's *Sentimental Excursions to Windsor, and Other Places* (1781) – unfairly accused by Oates of '[reducing] the brain to the consistency of damp flannel'[376] – was published in book-form, but first saw life as 'A Sentimental Excursion to Windsor', serialised in the *Public Ledger*. However, it was purloined by a rival newspaper, as the book's Advertisement states: 'This *Bagatelle* appeared originally in the PUBLIC LEDGER, in detached pieces, most

---

[373] *Sentimental Magazine* (November 1773), 390.
[374] Chandler, *Archaeology of Sympathy*, p. 194.
[375] *Gazetteer and New Daily Advertiser*, 17,710, 15 September 1785, 4, and 17,722, 29 September 1785, 3.
[376] Oates, *Shandyism*, p. 15.

of which were copied from that paper into the MORNING HERALD.———'.³⁷⁷ As we have seen, copying between press publications was standard, but the Advertisement frames the practice as parasitical in a way that exposes contemporary newspaper rivalries. The anti-Opposition *Morning Herald* was founded in November 1780 by the former editor of the *Morning Post*, the 'notorious' Reverend Henry Bate (Dudley).³⁷⁸ The *Public Ledger* was an Opposition paper.³⁷⁹ That 'A Sentimental Excursion to Windsor' was transplanted from its pages into the *Morning Herald* was potentially contentious – although the *Herald* also became an Opposition paper towards the end of 1783, indicative of newspapers' complicated political affiliations in this period.³⁸⁰ Leonard MacNally himself was the *Public Ledger*'s editor in the 1780s: he was well-placed to print his own fictional escapade to Windsor among its contents.

The excursion sees a listless narrator pursue a trip from London to Windsor, with encounters en route that provide opportunities to satirise sentimental journeys, including their erotic potential; stylistic traits and allusions link it to Sterne, alongside chapters titled (in the book version) 'A Shandean Conversation' and 'Tristram Shandy'; 'Slave Trade', first serialised in June 1781, re-contextualises its Sternean content to address contemporary issues, here, Abolition (which it advocates).³⁸¹ MacNally's journey narrative gained wider circulation not only through the multiple venues of its appearance but also through contemporary reviews, which acted as peep-holes on Sterne's reception and on the wider literary market. In December 1781, the *Edinburgh Magazine* observed that among countless 'Shandean' sentimental journeys, 'the author of Excursions to Windsor stands forth an avowed disciple of the Sternian school; and seems ... to have imitated his master with some degree of success', illustrated by a typographically inventive excerpt.³⁸² MacNally's 'success' counterbalances a Sterneana-overload, as 'Imitations of the inimitable Tristram are become so frequent as to render the perusal of them to the last degree tedious and disgusting'. The accusation was borne out by the appearance of another 'Sentimental Excursion' in the *Morning Herald* in August and September 1783, which encompasses locations including Barnet, Dunstable, and St Albans, and topics as varied as religion, 'Prostitutes', the 'Street-Walker', and pick-pockets.³⁸³

---

³⁷⁷ MacNally, *Sentimental Excursions*, Advertisement [n.p.].
³⁷⁸ Barker, *Newspapers*, p. 64; see also Ferrero, 'The *Morning Herald*', 166.
³⁷⁹ Ferrero, 'The *Morning Herald*', 167–8; Barker, *Newspapers*, p. 58, p. 61.
³⁸⁰ Barker, *Newspapers*, pp. 63–4, p. 52; Ferrero, 'The *Morning Herald*', 172.
³⁸¹ *Morning Herald*, 197, 18 June 1781, 3; *Morning Herald*, 202, 23 June 1781, 3; MacNally, *Sentimental Excursions*, pp. 219–27.
³⁸² *Edinburgh Magazine*, 54 (27 December 1781), 379–81.
³⁸³ *Morning Herald*, 883, 27 August 1783, 3, and subsequently.

Both MacNally's 'Sentimental Excursion' and this later version exploit the erotic possibilities of travel, especially of 'touching' sentimental journeys, an impetus others adopted, too. The tale of one 'sentimental sailor' in the *Town and Country Magazine* in January 1781 capitalises on maritime stereotypes to satirise sensibility as a performance learned from bad reading.[384] As Will Steerwell explains of Jack Tightcord's 'whining way of talking', apparently 'he was bit by a dog called Tristram Shandy, while blubbering o'er a book', which left Jack 'strangely altered'. His account of a coach journey proves the charge of sentimental hypocrisy, as 'the Great Fountain of Sensibility' inspires 'frolics' with a beautiful young woman, although an incredulous Tom Anchorstock tells him that '—Not both you and Beelzebub your brother, cousin Yorick, uncle Toby, and all the troop' will lure them to understand the nature of his temptations.

These journey narratives draw on both *A Sentimental Journey* and *Tristram Shandy*, and on the general perception of Sterne as an author who combined erotic humour, pathos, and narrative innovation in templates that could be remodelled in new ventures, aided by the serialisation nurtured by newspapers and magazines. Very rapidly, though, as the *Edinburgh Magazine*'s review of MacNally's *Excursion* suggests, the content and generic labelling of Sterne's sentimental journey – combined with 'the Shandean stile' – had become patterns for both novelty and repetition. For the *Cornwall Gazette* in August 1812, Sterne was identifiable with over-used sentimental markers, where just a word sufficed to provoke hackneyed recognition; 'sentimental writers ... are forever selecting smaller objects (like their master, Sterne)— some poor negro wench, crack-brained Maria, caged starling, or dead ass—and so dressing up their favorite object to the fancy and feelings of their reader', a pooh-poohing of Sternean tags that furnishes a proto-anti-woke attack on the rival Liberal newspaper, the Truro-based *West Briton*.[385]

By 1819, in reviewing Charles Matthews's 'At Home' one-man mimic-show at the English Opera House, the *Literary Gazette* suggests that the pathos popularised by well-known Sternean episodes had reproduced tiresome clichés; Matthews's journey to Paris takes in Boulogne, Montreuil, and 'Sterne's Nampont, which has received more celebrity from *one dead ass*, than other towns receive from *hundreds of living ones!*'[386] Sterne himself had become a tourist attraction by this point; John Poole's popular farcical stage character, Paul Pry, gains afterlife in a travel narrative printed in the *Westmoreland Gazette* in 1826 that takes him to Calais. At 'Dessin's hotel'

---

[384] *Town and Country Magazine*, 13 (January 1781), 35–9.
[385] *Cornwall Gazette*, 475, 1 August 1812, 4.
[386] *Literary Gazette*, 3.112 (13 March 1819), 172–3; see also *Edinburgh Magazine*, 1 (April 1819), 371.

a room labelled 'Sterne's chamber' was supposed to have lodged the author, but 'there is nothing to remind us of Yorick but a dirty mezzotint portrait of him'; the 'imposture' of exploitative Sterne-tourism diminishes the fond 'recollections' of his much-loved journey, and riles Pry, who sarcastically imagines enquiring after the dead ass at Nampont.[387] 'Sterne' had become an old chestnut, his celebrity and that of his writings generating trite that, nonetheless, confirmed the genuine admiration both author and works persistently inspired against the kitsch efforts of those who capitalised on his fame.

5 Conclusion: Creating Classics through the Press

In November 1822, a contributor self-styled 'Janus Weathercock' published 'The Academy of Taste for Grown Gentlemen, or the Infant Connoisseur's Go-Cart' in the *London Magazine*.[388] It declares its Shandean credentials from the outset with two epigraphs: one from *Tristram Shandy*, and the second from '*Tristram Shandy again*'. Sternean humour, self-reflexive gestures, freewheeling allusions, and dashes and asterisks bear out the trail of influence. But Sterne is not the only focus. What promises to be the first in a sequence of essays is quickly unpromised: 'No. I, *not* to be continued', a jibe at serialisation practices and at magazine culture more widely also reminiscent of the apparent invitation for continuation proffered by *Tristram Shandy*'s inconclusive narrative, and by *A Sentimental Journey*'s open-ended 'END'. Contemporaneous references, meanwhile – to Byron and Keats, for instance – pull this Shandean parody into a new time and place. Sterne, once more, is both a focal-point and a point of departure, lending a style to an ironical writer who inhabits his own contemporary moment, part-founded on past literary sensations that still seem to retain currency.

The Sternean brand continued to hold sway long after the furore surrounding *Tristram Shandy*'s first appearance and Sterne's sudden celebrity, but it also developed, as new publications appeared and as Sterne's authorial identity became modified in critical and public perceptions, partly in tandem with broader shifts in the literary landscape. Sterne was increasingly entrenched in a widespread move to consolidate a 'national library' of novelists, if not unproblematically. A major factor in the fluctuating coinage of the idea of what 'Sterne' signified, and in the author's incorporation into an increasingly sophisticated literary-critical discourse, was the frequency of press titles that critically reviewed and printed excerpts that recirculated Sterne's texts, but which also provided a vast platform for creative reactions in all their varieties,

---

[387] *Westmoreland Gazette*, 396, 8 April 1826, 1.
[388] *London Magazine*, 6.35 (November 1822), 445.

from passing allusions to serialised prose narratives, and which, in turn, shaped Sterne's reception. The rapidity of production and breadth of dissemination, and the inter-borrowing of press publications, helped to spread his presence across geographical and temporal borders, aided by a sizeable number of reader-contributors, named and unnamed, with differing motivations for participating in this network of criticism and of creativity, confirming Alan B. Howes's claim that no other author was mentioned in the press over such a long period, or as heterogeneously.[389]

This Element has unearthed much new material supporting this assertion, and provided some routes towards synthesising it, to enrich and partly to modify accounts of Sterne's reception, as well as opening up points of comparison with other creators and publications. Its findings also provoke methodological questions about the types of material that have typically been used to construct such narratives: newspapers and magazines have often ceded in significance to books, and even apparently ephemeral pamphlets. Indeed, one essayist writing with whimsical self-reflexivity in the *London Magazine* in 1828 wryly reinforces this notion in observing that 'during the popularity of Tristram Shandy, nothing was bought, or thought of, but humorous productions' – a direct result of the influence of booksellers, who 'make not only our books, but our authors', and dictate the form, contents, and style of new works according to what is likely to sell: '"We want nothing now but humour," said the booksellers, "there is no demand in the trade for any thing else".'[390] The breadth of material drawn from press publications in this study, and the conclusions that evolve from it, suggest the equally, if not more significant role they played in shaping Sterne's eventual establishment as an author of note. The neglect this material has historically – if not more recently – encountered, if dismissed as merely ephemeral, resonates with some eighteenth-century perceptions of the lesser status of these publications, and of the authors who contributed to them; as the *St James's Magazine* suggests in 1762, 'booksellers have erected themselves into proper and sufficient judges of all literary merit' such that 'an author, who writes so *apparently* under their colours, as the unfortunate word MAGAZINE seems to intimate, cannot hope to be considered in any other light than as their journeyman book-maker'.[391]

Beyond Sterne, the reception of other authors and well-known works may well acquire new dimensions if attention shifts from predominantly book-title resources to the press publications that are much vaster, and perhaps trickier to navigate, with significant consequences for understanding eighteenth-century

---

[389] Howes, *Yorick and the Critics*, p. 1.   [390] *London Magazine*, 2.9 (December 1828), 632.
[391] *St James's Magazine*, 1 (September 1762), 'To the Reader' [n.p.].

literary and (as James Raven demonstrates) publishing cultures.[392] Taking into fuller account the role of periodicals, newspapers, and magazines in fostering critical discourse and a sense of literary agency creates a more complicated, but richer picture of eighteenth-century cultural life. Named authorship and anonymity cohabited simultaneously in the pages of press titles that, on the one hand, contributed towards the canonisation of celebrated writers, shaping public opinion about who to read and why they might be considered significant, and, on the other, provided a fertile space for unnamed members of the virtual communities created by press publications to participate in textual productivity, often by responding creatively to the productions of those authors of note.

This Element's focus on Sterne has inevitably promoted his reception as a special case, while suggesting ways in which, as a case study, it parallels or opens up enquiry into other authors' reception, or wider literary cultures. But was Sterne really more prominent than others, or considered more 'inimitable'? Is the extensiveness of the critical and creative reactions forming his reception, as recorded in the press, unique, or was it typical? Of the best-selling novelists of 1750–69 – who, following Michael F. Suarez, included Henry Fielding, Eliza Haywood, Tobias Smollett, and Samuel Richardson – a test-search of the datasets for the newspapers, magazines, and periodicals operating during this period yields fewer mentions compared with Sterne's, usually allied to advertisements for and reviews of their publications; indeed, Sterne tops Suarez's list of best-sellers.[393] A similar search for best-sellers during the larger time-span covered by this Element presents comparable results.[394] References to Sterne and his fictions endured well beyond the immediate moment of his initial literary fame and commercial success, often at unexpected points; indeed, according to *British Library Newspapers* frequency graphs, 'Sterne' peaks in 1794 and 1807, years not particularly significant for his publications themselves. By contrast, some authors arguably experienced a fading away. Kit Kincaide, for instance, writes of Defoe's declining appearance in the later eighteenth century that in a piece published in 1785 the *Gentleman's Magazine* only 'vaguely recollected' that he was the author of *Robinson Crusoe*.[395] Although far from thoroughly scientific, such an exercise suggests some ways in which to discern patterns of authorial reception in the press, and where to position Sterne.

The variety of Sterne's published output, and the complexity of its style (mixing humour, pathos, and wit), marked him out as, in many respects unique, and inimitable – as contemporary reviewers of his works, and of ever-emerging 'Imitations of the inimitable Tristram', consistently commented.[396] This lexical

---
[392] Raven, *Publishing Business*, pp. 52–4. [393] Suarez, 'Business of Fiction', pp. 27–8.
[394] Raven, *Business of Books*, pp. 224–5. [395] Kincade, 'Defoe's Critical Reception', p. 613.
[396] *Edinburgh Magazine*, 54 (December 1781), 379.

lodestone was not unique to Sterne: in the period covered by this Element, 'inimitable' is regularly applied to authors from Molière to Pope, as it would later be to Dickens; other authors gained similar titles, such as 'the incomparable Smollett' celebrated by the *Weekly Entertainer*.[397] Nonetheless, in Sterne's case, the label was attached almost from the outset, and was repeatedly deployed as one gauge by which to assess not only Sterne and his imitators, but also the wider field of contemporary fiction, and its claims to novelty. Were they truly original, or did they pretend to originality by aping the most inimitable 'original'?

Sterne was clearly not alone in creating inviting models for imitation – as suggested, literary reception in this period was strongly marked by critical-creative adaptation. Indeed, a review of the epistolary novel *Love at First Sight* in the *Monthly Review* in 1773 identifies a cluster of well-known authors as particularly susceptible to the mass-imitation that popularity and success seem to breed; the reviewer (alluding to *Tristram Shandy*) claims that 'Paper-makers and printers certainly owe some public monument of gratitude to the memories of Fielding, Richardson, and Sterne, for the amazing consumption of paper and print the numerous imitations of their patterns have occasioned within the last twenty years'.[398] Like the cut-out 'pattern' followed by a seamstress, these celebrated figures seemed to offer clear lines for future creators, but whose endeavours were inevitably always compared back to the model rather than being considered innovative or distinctive. In Sterne's case, there seemed to be something that made him impossible to ape without the imitation being pejoratively detected, but as suggested in this study the 'patterns' of his writing encompassed more than one predominant mode or style, arguably more evidently than these famous contemporaries.

In evaluating how far Sterne was '*inimitable*', and his wider authorial status, the *Critical Review* concluded even in February 1766 that his style is as elusive as 'the clouds of last year' and escapes emulation: 'here we have him, there we have him, and we have him no where', a judgement based on eight volumes of *Tristram Shandy* and four of sermons.[399] By October 1785, when 'Eugenius' pseudonymously authored 'On the Imitators of Sterne' in the *General Evening Post*, the Sternean corpus and the author's reputation were even more firmly in place against a backdrop of shifting literary modes. Eugenius positions Sterne as inadvertently responsible for a host of poor copies, especially in the sentimental vein: 'the imitators of the inimitable *Sterne*' over-use a codified system of sentimentalised clichés.[400] Eugenius identifies press publications as

---

[397] *Weekly Entertainer*, 12.303, 6 January 1787, 397–8.
[398] *Monthly Review*, 48 (February 1773), 155; cf. Sterne, *Tristram Shandy*, vol. 1, p. 342.
[399] *Critical Review*, 21 (February 1766), 141.
[400] *General Evening Post*, 8110, 13–15 October 1785, 2.

particularly guilty of providing a space for such imitators, as 'periodical publications, within these last ten years, have teemed with *titulary marks* as the *signposts* of sentiment'. These stylistic traits are difficult to replicate without becoming trite, and 'a manner of writing so peculiar and excentric as that of *Sterne's*' marks out his 'genius' as unique: 'no writer ... can give the faintest imitation of *Sterne*'.[401] Clara Reeve's literary-critical account of prose fiction, *The History of Romance*, was published in the same year; while sceptical of *Tristram Shandy*'s faddish appeal, she nonetheless praises *A Sentimental Journey*'s pathos, and already situates Sterne in a pantheon of notable authors marked out as 'Original' partly because of the unsuccessful 'swarm of imitators' who, unlike their model, do not 'deserve mention among works of eminence in this class of writing'.[402] By 1813, 'On the Writings and Style of Sterne' in the *Lady's Monthly Museum* further confirms this status: 'Nothing so much shews the excellence of an author, as the inferiority of his imitators; what a train of writers have succeeded Sterne!', although most readers will easily 'distinguish between his genius and wit, and the puny, awkward attempts of his copyists'.[403] The industry of attempting to imitate Sterne not only endured, but became at once more attractive and more challenging the more his claims to 'genius' became established in critical and public discourse.

The difficulties of Sterne's inimitably were mixed with his perhaps unique, partially self-forged literary celebrity, and its embeddedness in the production and reception of his writings. The press's role not only in facilitating but in shaping that popular and critical identity sat within these publications' wider function in spreading and amplifying celebrity cultures more generally, especially literary ones. While Sterne offers a distinctive case study, the press machinery that shaped his reception in critical and creative ways, of course, also disseminated others' celebrity identities – and confirmed both their canonical significance and their presence in the popular consciousness, recalling David Brewer's argument that academic and social canons were entwined through patterns of adaptation; the press, as a major conduit for networks based on production, consumption, and recirculation inextricably cemented both canons.[404] Eighteenth-century literary culture, in other words, was transformed by a mechanism of publication that seemed ephemerally removed from more prestigious book publications, and yet which anchored the 'classic' significance of many authors in ways that continue to impact literary history, in Britain and in wider European cultures.[405] Critical appraisals of Sterne participated in larger movements towards identifying 'major' British authors, especially in the increasingly appreciated domain of

---

[401] Newbould, *Adaptations*, pp. 104–5. [402] Reeve, *Progress*, vol. 2, p. 31.
[403] *Lady's Monthly Museum*, 15 (September 1813), 134–7. [404] Brewer, *Afterlife*, p. 17.
[405] Raven, *Publishing Business*, p. 53.

prose fiction. Advertisements, reviews, and excerpts in the press emerged alongside collected works and anthologies of famous writers that helped to reshape existing categories of 'genius' in the services of a national literature. Sterne took his place as a classic author representative of a peculiarly British way of writing, idiosyncratic and yet elusively methodical, marginally 'outré', but nonetheless in some way fundamentally grasping a way of being in his writing that resonated with a perceived national identity. By 1798, one essayist in the *Journal de Paris* places Sterne on a list of significant authors – Lucian, Erasmus, Montaigne, Rabelais, Swift, Bayle, and Montesquieu – in addressing the question '*A-t-il existé un vrai génie ?*'[406] A newspaper that sustained strong links with British counterparts, the *Journal* shows that the network of associations in which Sterne's reputation and reception were forged involved cross-cultural conversations, in which one nation's approach towards understanding and confirming its national literature was in part shaped by appreciating that of another. Newspapers, periodicals, and magazines significantly sustained the momentum of Sterne's continuing presence in these discourses both by consolidating critical assessments of his work as deserving serious attention, and by recirculating the very varied creative reinterpretations his mixed output inspired for many years.

In August 1823 the *Leeds Intelligencer*, reviewing volume 5 of Ballantyne's Novelist's Library, which packaged together *Tristram Shandy* and *A Sentimental Journey* with a preface by Walter Scott, identifies Sterne as among 'the most popular British classics', his works granted an acknowledged place in a national pantheon to which only 'the most powerful and universal genius of the day' could pay tribute: Scott, as the most successful contemporary novelist but also a renowned critic. Sterne, with the volume's other authors – Goldsmith, Johnson, Mackenzie, Walpole, Reeve – set a pattern for critical assessment and for future creative inspiration, even accounting for the 'borrowed materials' unearthed by Ferriar. A lengthy excerpt from Scott's introduction to Sterne offers the newspaper's readers the takeaway message that he stands out as unique: in touching pathos, he has 'never been excelled', and Sterne remains 'one of the most original geniuses, whom England has produced'.[407]

---

[406] *Journal de Paris*, 147, 15 February 1798, 4.
[407] *Leeds Intelligencer*, 3,607, 21 August 1823, 4.

Bibliography

Periodicals, Newspapers, and Magazines

Annales typographiques, ou notice du progrès des connoissances humaines
The Annual Register
The Beauties of All the Magazines Selected
The Boston Magazine
The British Chronicle, or Pugh's Hereford Journal
The British Magazine; or Monthly Repository for Gentlemen and Ladies
The Caledonian Mercury
The Calcutta Journal of Politics and General Literature
The Chester Chronicle
The Cornwall Gazette
The Country Constitutional Guardian and Literary Magazine
The Craftsman; or Say's Weekly Journal
The Critical Review, or, Annals of Literature
The Dublin Mercury
The Edinburgh Magazine
The English Chronicle, or Universal Evening-Post
The Evening Fire-Side
The Gazetteer and New Daily Advertiser
The General Evening Post
The Genius
The Gentleman's Magazine
The Grand Magazine
Le Journal de Paris
The Lady's Magazine (1759–63)
The Lady's Magazine (1770–1832)
The Lady's Monthly Museum
The Leeds Intelligencer, and Yorkshire General Advertiser
The Literary Gazette: A Weekly Journal of Literature, Science, and the Fine Arts
The London Chronicle: or, Universal Evening Post
The London Evening-Post
The London Magazine, or, Gentleman's Monthly Intelligencer
The Manchester and Liverpool Museum: Or, the Beauties of All Magazines Selected
The Manchester Mercury and Harrop's General Advertiser
The Monitor, or British Freeholder
The Monthly Miscellany

The Monthly Review
The Monthly Visitor, and Pocket Companion
The Morning Herald, and Daily Advertiser
The Morning Post, and Daily Advertiser
The New Lady's Magazine
The New Monthly Magazine
The Oxford Magazine, or, Universal Museum
The Political Register; and Impartial Review of New Books
The Public Advertiser
The Public Ledger
The Scots Magazine
The Sentimental Magazine
The St James's Chronicle
The St James's Magazine
The Theatre
The Thespian Mirror
The Town and Country Magazine; or, Universal Repository of Knowledge, Instruction, and Entertainment
The Universal Magazine of Knowledge and Pleasure
The Universal Museum, or Gentleman's & Ladies Polite Magazine
The Universal Review: or Critical Commentary on the Literary Productions of these Kingdoms
Walker's Hibernian Magazine
The Weekly Entertainer; or, Agreeable and Instructive Repository
The Weekly Miscellany: Or, Instructive Entertainer
The Westmoreland Gazette, and Kendal Advertiser
The Whitehall Evening Post

Primary and Secondary Material

Anderson, Jocelyn, 'Eighteenth-Century Magazine Illustration and Copper Plates Coloured from Nature', *Lumen*, 39 (2020), 79–111. https://doi.org/10.7202/1069405ar.

Anonymous, *The Letters of Maria; to Which is Added, an Account of Her Death* (London: G. Kearsley, 1790).

Ballaster, Rosalind, Margaret Beetham, Elizabeth Frazer, and Sarah Hebron, *Women's Worlds: Ideology, Femininity and the Woman's Magazine* (London: Macmillan, 1991).

Bandry, Anne, 'Les faux volumes de *Tristram Shandy*', *XVII–XVIII. Bulletin de la société d'études anglo-américaines des XVIIe et XVIIIe siècles*, 36 (1993), 25–42.

Bandry, Anne, *Tristram Shandy: Créations et imitations en Angleterre au XVIIIe Siècle*, Thèse à l'Université de la Sorbonne, Paris III (1991).

Bandry, Anne, '*Tristram Shandy*, the *Public Ledger*, and William Dodd', *Eighteenth-Century Fiction*, 14.3–4 (2002), 311–24.

Bandry-Scubbi, Anne, 'Sterne recyclé: allers-retours entre culture savante et culture populaire', *Recherches anglaises et nord-américaines*, 43 (2010), 13–23.

Bandry-Scubbi, Anne, 'The Visitor, the Inspectress, Selima, Obadiah et Tristram, ou comment s'anime le *Public Ledger* en 1760–1761', *XVII–XVIII. Bulletin de la société d'études anglo-américaines des XVIIe et XVIIIe siècles*, 50 (2000), 283–98.

Barchas, Janine, *Graphic Design, Print Culture, and the Eighteenth-Century Novel* (Cambridge: Cambridge University Press, 2003).

Barker, Hannah, *Newspapers, Politics and English Society, 1695–1855* (Harlow: Longman, 2000).

Barker-Benfield, G. J., *Ignatius Sancho and the British Abolitionist Movement, 1729–1786: Manhood, Race and Sensibility* (Basingstoke: Palgrave Macmillan, 2023).

Barnett, George L., 'Gay, Swift, and "Tristram Shandy"', *Notes & Queries*, 185.12 (1943), 346–7.

Batchelor, Jennie, '"Connections, which are of service ... in a more advanced age": *The Lady's Magazine*, Community, and Women's Literary Histories', *Tulsa Studies in Women's Literature*, 30.2 (2011), 245–67.

Batchelor, Jennie, *The 'Lady's Magazine' (1770–1832) and the Making of Literary History* (Edinburgh: Edinburgh University Press, 2022).

Batchelor, Jennie, and Manushag N. Powell, 'Introduction: Women and the Birth of Periodical Culture', in Jennie Batchelor and Manushag N. Powell (eds.), *Women's Periodicals and Print Culture in Britain, 1690–1820s: The Long Eighteenth Century* (Edinburgh: Edinburgh University Press, 2018), pp. 1–19.

Black, Jeremy, *The English Press in the Eighteenth Century* (Aldershot: Croom Helm, 1987; repr. Brookfield: Gregg Revivals, 1991).

Bosch, René, *Labyrinth of Digressions: 'Tristram Shandy' as Perceived and Influenced by Sterne's Early Imitators*, trans. Piet Verhoeff (Amsterdam and New York: Rodopi, 2007).

Braber, Helleke van den, Jeroen Dera, Jos Joosten, and, Maarten Steenmeijer, 'Introduction', in Helleke van den Braber, Jeroen Dera, Jos Joosten, and Maarten Steenmeijer (eds.), *Branding Books Across the Ages: Strategies and Key Concepts in Literary Branding* (Amsterdam: Amsterdam University Press, 2021), pp. 9–29.

Brandtzæg, Siv Gøril, M-C. Newbould, and Helen Williams, 'Advertising Sterne's Novels in Eighteenth-Century Newspapers', *The Shandean*, 27 (2016), 27–55.

Brandtzæg, Siv Gøril, Paul Goring, and Christine Watson (eds.), *Travelling Chronicles: News and Newspapers from the Early Modern Period to the Eighteenth Century* (Leiden: Brill, 2018).

Brewer, David A., *The Afterlife of Character, 1726–1825* (Delaware: University of Pennsylvania Press, 2005).

Brewer, David A., 'The Tactility of Authorial Names', *The Eighteenth Century*, 54.2 (2013), 195–213. https://doi.org/10.1353/ecy.2013.0019.

Cash, Arthur H., *Laurence Sterne: The Later Years* (London: Methuen, 1986).

Chandler, James, *An Archaeology of Sympathy: The Sentimental Mode in Literature and Cinema* (Chicago; London: University of Chicago Press, 2013).

[Combe, William], *Sterne's Letters to His Friends on Various Occasions; to which is Added, His History of a Watch Coat, with Explanatory Notes* (London: G. Kearsly, 1775).

Cook, Daniel, 'Authors Unformed: Reading "Beauties" in the Eighteenth Century', *Philological Quarterly*, 89 (2010), 283–309.

Cook, Daniel, 'Further Voyages', in Daniel Cook and Nicholas Seager (eds.), *The Cambridge Companion to Gulliver's Travels* (Cambridge: Cambridge University Press, 2023), pp. 192–205.

Cook, Daniel, and Nicholas Seager, 'Introduction', in Daniel Cook and Nicholas Seager (eds.), *The Afterlives of Eighteenth-Century Fiction* (Cambridge: Cambridge University Press, 2015), pp. 1–19.

Deleuze, Gilles, and Félix Guattari, *A Thousand Plateaus: Capitalism and Schizophrenia*, trans. Brian Massumi (London: Continuum, repr. 2004).

DiPlacidi, Jenny, '"Full of pretty stories": Fiction in the *Lady's Magazine* (1770–1832)', in Jennie Batchelor and Manushag N. Powell (eds.), *Women's Periodicals and Print Culture in Britain, 1690–1820s: The Long Eighteenth Century* (Edinburgh: Edinburgh University Press, 2018), pp. 263–77.

Donoghue, Frank, *The Fame Machine: Book Reviewing and Eighteenth-Century Literary Careers* (Stanford: Stanford University Press, 1996).

Elliott, Kamilla, *Theorizing Adaptation* (Oxford: Oxford University Press, 2020).

Ellis, Markman, 'Poetry and Civic Urbanism in the Coffee-House Library in the Mid-Eighteenth Century', in Mark Towsey and Kyle B. Roberts (eds.), *Before the Public Library: Reading, Community and Identity in the Atlantic World, 1650–1850* (Leiden: Brill, 2017), pp. 52–72.

Ezell, Margaret J. M., *Early English Periodicals and Early Modern Social Media* (Cambridge: Cambridge University Press, 2024).

Fairer, David, 'Introduction: "All Managed for the Best": Ecology and the Dynamics of Adaptation', in Kevin L. Cope and Samara Anne Cahill (eds.), *Citizens of the World: Adapting in the Eighteenth Century* (Lewisburg: Bucknell University Press, 2015), pp. xxv–xlviii.

Ferdinand, C. Y., *Benjamin Collins and the Provincial Newspaper Trade in the Eighteenth Century* (Oxford: Clarendon, 1997).

Fergus, Jan S., *Provincial Readers in Eighteenth-Century England* (Oxford: Oxford University Press, 2006).

Ferrero, Bonnie, 'The *Morning Herald* and its First Three Editors', *Media History*, 11.3 (2005), 165–75. https://doi.org/10.1080/13688800500323865.

Ferriar, John, 'Comments on Sterne', *Memoirs of the Manchester Literary and Philosophical Society*, 4.1 (1793), 45–86.

Gallagher, Catherine, *Nobody's Story: The Vanishing Acts of Women Writers in the Marketplace, 1670–1820* (Berkeley: University of California Press, 1995).

Gerard, W. B., *Laurence Sterne and the Visual Imagination* (Aldershot and Burlington: Ashgate, 2006).

Gerard, W. B., 'Laurence Sterne, the Apostrophe, and American Abolitionism, 1788–1831', in W. B. Gerard, E. Derek Taylor, and Robert G. Walker (eds.), *Swiftly Sterneward: Essays on Laurence Sterne and His Times in Honor of Melvyn New* (Newark: University of Delaware Press, 2011), pp. 181–206.

Goring, Paul, 'Authorial Authority and the Mapping of an -ana', *1650–1850: Ideas, Aesthetics, and Inquiries in the Early Modern Era*, 28 (2023), 181–98.

Goring, Paul, 'The Evolution of "A Sentimental Journey, by a Lady" in *The Lady's Magazine*', *The Shandean*, 31 (2020), 67–100.

Goring, Paul, 'A Network of Networks: Spreading the News in an Expanding World of Information', in Siv Gøril Brandtzæg, Paul Goring, and Christine Watson (eds.), *Travelling Chronicles: News and Newspapers from the Early Modern Period to the Eighteenth Century* (Leiden: Brill, 2018), pp. 1–23.

Goring, Paul, 'Notes on a (Currently) Lost Pamphlet by Samuel Paterson', *The Shandean*, 33 (2022), 273–84.

Hartvig, Gabriella, 'Advertising Sterne's Letters in the 1770s', *The Shandean*, 34–35 (2024), 63–86.

Havard, John Owen, 'Only Disconnect? Laurence Sterne, Politics, and the Public', in Ileana Baird (ed.), *Social Networks in the Long Eighteenth Century: Clubs, Literary Salons, Textual Coteries* (Newcastle: Cambridge Scholars Publishing, 2014), pp. 267–90.

Heyd, Uriel, 'Fifteen Lines of Fame: Theatrical Representations of Eighteenth-Century Celebrity and the Press', in Ileana Baird (ed.), *Social Networks in the Long Eighteenth Century: Clubs, Literary Salons, Textual Coteries* (Newcastle: Cambridge Scholars Publishing, 2014), pp. 99–120.

Heyd, Uriel, 'News Craze: Public Sphere and the Eighteenth-Century Theatrical Depiction of Newspaper Culture', *The Eighteenth Century*, 56.1 (2015), 59–84.

Howes, Alan B., *Sterne: The Critical Heritage* (London and Boston: Routledge and Kegan Paul, 1974).

Howes, Alan B., *Yorick and the Critics: Sterne's Reputation in England, 1760–1868* (Hamden: Archon, 1971).

Hutcheon, Linda, with Siobhan O'Flynn, *A Theory of Adaptation*, 2nd ed. (London and New York: Routledge, 2013).

Jones, Emrys D., and Victoria Joule (eds.), *Intimacy and Celebrity in Eighteenth-Century Literary Culture: Public Interiors* (Basingstoke, Hampshire: Palgrave Macmillan, 2018).

Keymer, Thomas, 'Small Particles of Fame: Subjectivity, Celebrity, Sterne', in Melvyn New, Peter de Voogd, and Judith Hawley (eds.), *Sterne, Tristram, Yorick: Tercentenary Essays on Laurene Sterne* (Newark: University of Delaware Press, 2016), pp. 3–24.

Keymer, Thomas, *Sterne, the Moderns, and the Novel* (Oxford: Oxford University Press, 2002).

Keymer, Thomas, and Peter Sabor, *'Pamela' in the Marketplace: Literary Controversy and Print Culture in Eighteenth-Century Britain and Ireland* (Cambridge: Cambridge University Press, 2005).

Kincade, Kit, 'Defoe's Critical Reception, 1731–1945', in Nicholas Seager and J. A. Downie (eds.), *The Oxford Handbook of Daniel Defoe* (Oxford: Oxford University Press, 2023), pp. 610–23.

Lipski, Jakub, 'Introduction', in Jakub Lipski (ed.), *Rewriting Crusoe: The Robinsonade across Languages, Cultures, and Media* (Lewisburg: Bucknell University Press, 2020), pp. 1–6.

Lupton, Christina, *Reading and the Making of Time in the Eighteenth Century* (Baltimore: John Hopkins University Press, 2018).

MacNally, Leonard, *Sentimental Excursions to Windsor and Other Places, with Notes Critical, Illustrative, and Explanatory* (London: J. Walker, 1781).

Mayo, Robert D., *The English Novel in the Magazines, 1740–1815: With a Catalogue of 1375 Magazine Novels and Novelettes* (Evanston: Northwestern University Press; Oxford: Oxford University Press, 1962).

McDowell, Paula, 'Of Grubs and Other Insects: Constructing the Categories of "Ephemera" and "Literature" in Eighteenth-Century British Writing', in

Kevin Murphy and Sally O'Driscoll (eds.), *Studies in Ephemera: Text and Image in Eighteenth-Century Print* (Lewisburg: Bucknell University Press, 2013), pp. 31–53.

Mitchell, Eleanor Drake, 'The Tête-À-Têtes in the "Town and Country Magazine" (1769–1793)', *Interpretations*, 9.1 (1977), 12–21.

Moretti, Franco, 'Network Theory, Plot Analysis', *New Left Review*, 68 (2011), 80–102.

Murray, Simone, *The Adaptation Industry: The Cultural Economy of Contemporary Literary Adaptation* (London and New York: Routledge, 2012).

New, Melvyn, 'Pots and Kettles: William Dodd on Sterne', *The Shandean*, 29 (2018), 141–4.

Newbould, M-C., *Adaptations of Laurene Sterne's Fiction: Sterneana, 1760–1840* (Farnham: Ashgate, 2013).

Newbould, M-C., '"[It] Were Wisdome It Selfe, to Read All Authors, as *Anonymo's*": Anonymity, Virtual Communities, and Sterneana', *1650–1850: Ideas, Aesthetics, and Inquiries in the Early Modern Era*, 28 (2023), 163–80.

Newbould, M-C., 'Wit and Humour for the Heart of Sensibility: The Beauties of Fielding and Sterne', in Daniel Cook and Nicholas Seager (eds.), *The Afterlives of Eighteenth-Century Fiction* (Cambridge: Cambridge University Press, 2015), pp. 133–52.

Newbould, M-C., and Helen Williams, 'Literary Adaptation and Digital Humanities: Laurence Sterne and Sterneana', *Studies in Romanticism*, 63.3 (Fall 2024), 273–302.

Nicklas, Pascal, and Oliver Lindner, 'Adaptation and Cultural Appropriation', in Pascal Nicklas and Oliver Lindner (eds.), *Adaptation and Cultural Appropriation: Literature, Film, and the Arts* (Berlin; Boston: De Gruyter, 2012), pp. 1–13.

Oakley, Warren L., *A Culture of Mimicry: Laurence Sterne, His Readers and the Art of Bodysnatching*, rev. ed. (Abingdon: Routledge, 2017).

Oates, J. C. T., *Shandyism and Sentiment, 1760–1800* (Cambridge: Cambridge Bibliographical Society Publications, 1968).

Parnell, Tim, 'Sterne's Fiction and the Mid-Century Novel: The "Vast Empire of Biographical Freebooters" and the "Crying Volume"', in James Alan Downie (ed.), *The Oxford Handbook of the Eighteenth-Century Novel* (Oxford: Oxford University Press, 2016), pp. 264–81.

Pettegree, Andrew, *Brand Luther: 1517, Printing, and the Making of the Reformation* (New York: Penguin Press, 2015).

Pierce, David, and Peter de Voogd (eds.), *Laurence Sterne in Modernism and Postmodernism* (Amsterdam: Rodopi, 1996).

Powell, Manushag N., *Performing Authorship in Eighteenth-Century English Periodicals* (Lewisburg: Bucknell University Press, 2012).

Prescott, Andrew, 'Searching for Dr. Johnson: The Digitisation of the Burney Newspaper Collection', in Siv Gøril Brandtzæg, Paul Goring, and Christine Watson (eds.), *Travelling Chronicles: News and Newspapers from the Early Modern Period to the Eighteenth Century* (Leiden: Brill, 2018), pp. 51–71.

Raven, James, *The Business of Books: Booksellers and the English Book Trade, 1450–1850* (New Haven; London: Yale University Press, 2007).

Raven, James, *Judging New Wealth: Popular Publishing and Responses to Commerce in England, 1750–1800* (Oxford: Clarendon, 1992).

Raven, James, *Publishing Business in Eighteenth-Century England* (Woodbridge: Boydell & Brewer, 2014).

Raven, James, 'Serial Advertisement in 18th-Century Britain and Ireland', in Robin Myers and Michael Harris (eds.), *Serials and Their Readers, 1620–1914* (Winchester: St. Paul's; Newcastle: Oak Knoll Press, 1993), pp. 103–22.

Reeve, Clara, *The Progress of Romance, through Times, Countries, and Manners*, 2 vols (Colchester: W. Keymer, 1785).

Regan, Shaun, 'Locating Richard Griffith: Genre, Nation, Canon', *Irish University Review*, 41.1 (2011), 95–114.

Regan, Shaun, 'The Posthumous Works of the Celebrated Dr. Sterne (Oates.417)', *Laurence Sterne and Sterneana*, Cambridge Digital Library. https://cudl.lib.cam.ac.uk/view/PR-OATES-00417/1.

Richardson, Samuel, *Correspondence with Lady Bradshaigh and Lady Echlin, 1748–1753*, ed. Peter Sabor (Cambridge: Cambridge University Press, 2016).

Richardson, Samuel, *Pamela: Or, Virtue Rewarded*, ed. Thomas Keymer (Oxford: Oxford University Press, 2001).

Seager, Nicholas, 'The Novel's Afterlife in the Newspaper, 1712–1750', in Daniel Cook and Nicholas Seager (eds.), *The Afterlives of Eighteenth-Century Fiction* (Cambridge: Cambridge University Press, 2015), pp. 111–32.

Solomon, Alex, 'The Anti-Slavery Legacy of the Sancho-Sterne Correspondence in the Periodical Press', *Rutgers.edu*. https://sancho.rutgers.edu/antislavery-legacy/.

Somers, Tim, *Ephemeral Print Culture in Early Modern England: Sociability, Politics and Collecting* (Woodbridge: Boydell Press, 2021).

Squires, Claire, *Marketing Literature: The Making of Contemporary Writing in Britain* (Basingstoke; New York: Palgrave Macmillan, 2007).

Sterne, Laurence, *Letters of the Late Rev. Mr. Laurence Sterne, to His Most Intimate Friends; with a Fragment in the Manner of Rabelais*, 3 vols (London: T. Becket, 1775).

Sterne, Laurence, *The Letters, Part 1: 1739–1764* and *The Letters, Part 2: 1765–1768*, ed. Melvyn New and Peter de Voogd, 2 vols (Gainesville: University Press of Florida, 2009).

Sterne, Laurence, *The Life and Opinions of Tristram Shandy, Gentleman*, ed. Melvyn New and Joan New, 2 vols (Gainesville: University Presses of Florida, 1978).

Sterne, Laurence, *The Miscellaneous Writings and Sterne's Subscribers, an Identification List*, ed. Melvyn New and W. B. Gerard (Gainesville: University Press of Florida, 2014).

Sterne, Laurence, *A Political Romance, Addressed To — — Esq. of York* (London: J. Murdoch, 1769).

Sterne, Laurence, *A Sentimental Journey through France and Italy and Continuation of the Bramine's Journal*, ed. Melvyn New and W. G. Day (Gainesville: University Press of Florida, 2002).

Suarez, Michael F., 'Business of Fiction: Novel Publishing, 1695–1774', in James Alan Downie (ed.), *The Oxford Handbook of the Eighteenth-Century Novel* (Oxford: Oxford University Press, 2016), pp. 22–38. https://doi.org/10.1093/oxfordhb/9780199566747.013.34.

Tremain, Catherine, 'Life after Death: Gender, Idealized Virtues, and the Obituary in Eighteenth-Century Newspapers', in Simon Davies and Puck Fletcher (eds.), *News in Early Modern Europe: Currents and Connections* (Leiden: Brill, 2014), pp. 175–95. https://doi-org.ezp.lib.cam.ac.uk/10.1163/9789004276864_011.

Vareschi, Mark, *Everywhere and Nowhere: Anonymity and Mediation in Eighteenth-Century Britain* (Minneapolis: University of Minnesota Press, 2018).

Voogd, Peter de, 'Sterne's letters to his friends on various occasions (Oates.385)', *Laurence Sterne and Sterneana*, Cambridge Digital Library. https://cudl.lib.cam.ac.uk/view/PR-OATES-00385/1.

Voogd, Peter de, and John Neubauer (eds.), *The Reception of Laurence Sterne in Europe* (London and New York: Thoemmes Continuum, 2004).

Williams, Abigail, *The Social Life of Books: Reading Together in the Eighteenth-Century Home* (New Haven and London: Yale University Press, 2017).

Williamson, Gillian, *British Masculinity in the 'Gentleman's Magazine', 1731 to 1815* (London: Palgrave Macmillan, 2016).

Acknowledgements

This research is part of the project No. 2021/43/P/HS2/01182 co-funded by the National Science Centre and the European Union Framework Programme for Research and Innovation Horizon 2020 under the Marie Skłodowska-Curie grant agreement No.945339. For the purpose of Open Access, the author has applied a CC-BY public copyright licence to any Author Accepted Manuscript (AAM) version arising from this submission.

I am grateful to Kazimierz Wielki University, Bydgoszcz, for hosting the project that gave rise to this Element, and particularly to Jakub Lipski for his ongoing support and judicious comments on the manuscript. My thanks also to Paul Goring, Peter de Voogd, and the two anonymous readers for their very helpful suggestions, and to Katrin Ettenhuber for her wise friendship. I add a final, personal word for Christine and Mike, Juliette and Jeff, and for Francesco Rognoni, to whom I dedicate this Element.

Cambridge Elements =

Eighteenth-Century Connections

Series Editors
Eve Tavor Bannet
University of Oklahoma

Eve Tavor Bannet is George Lynn Cross Professor Emeritus, University of Oklahoma and editor of *Studies in Eighteenth-Century Culture*. Her monographs include *Empire of Letters: Letter Manuals and Transatlantic Correspondence 1688–1820* (Cambridge, 2005), *Transatlantic Stories and the History of Reading, 1720–1820* (Cambridge, 2011), and *Eighteenth-Century Manners of Reading: Print Culture and Popular Instruction in the Anglophone Atlantic World* (Cambridge, 2017). She is editor of *British and American Letter Manuals 1680–1810* (Pickering & Chatto, 2008), *Emma Corbett* (Broadview, 2011) and, with Susan Manning, *Transatlantic Literary Studies* (Cambridge, 2012).

Markman Ellis
Queen Mary University of London

Markman Ellis is Professor of Eighteenth-Century Studies at Queen Mary University of London. He is the author of *The Politics of Sensibility: Race, Gender and Commerce in the Sentimental Novel* (1996), *The History of Gothic Fiction* (2000), *The Coffee-House: a Cultural History* (2004), and *Empire of Tea* (co-authored, 2015). He edited *Eighteenth-Century Coffee-House Culture* (4 vols, 2006) and *Tea and the Tea-Table in Eighteenth-Century England* (4 vols 2010), and co-editor of *Discourses of Slavery and Abolition* (2004) and *Prostitution and Eighteenth-Century Culture: Sex, Commerce and Morality* (2012).

Advisory Board
Linda Bree, *Independent*
Claire Connolly, *University College Cork*
Gillian Dow, *University of Southampton*
James Harris, *University of St Andrews*
Thomas Keymer, *University of Toronto*
Jon Mee, *University of York*
Carla Mulford, *Penn State University*
Nicola Parsons, *University of Sydney*
Manushag Powell, *Purdue University*
Robbie Richardson, *University of Kent*
Shef Rogers, *University of Otago*
Eleanor Shevlin, *West Chester University*
David Taylor, *Oxford University*
Chloe Wigston Smith, *University of York*
Roxann Wheeler, *Ohio State University*
Eugenia Zuroski, *MacMaster University*

About the Series
Exploring connections between verbal and visual texts and the people, networks, cultures and places that engendered and enjoyed them during the long Eighteenth Century, this innovative series also examines the period's uses of oral, written and visual media, and experiments with the digital platform to facilitate communication of original scholarship with both colleagues and students.

Cambridge Elements

Eighteenth-Century Connections

Elements in the Series

Pastoral Care through Letters in the British Atlantic
Alison Searle

The Domino and the Eighteenth-Century London Masquerade: A Social Biography of a Costume
Meghan Kobza

Paratext Printed with New English Plays, 1660–1700
Robert D. Hume

The Art of the Actress
Fashioning Identities

A Performance History of The Fair Penitent
Elaine McGirr

Labour of the Stitch: The Making and Remaking of Fashionable Georgian Dress
Serena Dyer

Early English Periodicals and Early Modern Social Media
Margaret J. M. Ezell

Reading with the Burneys: Patronage, Paratext, and Performance
Sophie Coulombeau

Jacobitism and Cultural Memory, 1688–1830
Leith Davis

On Wonder: Literature and Science in the Long Eighteenth Century
Tita Chico

The Epistemologies of Progress
Richard Adelman

Networks of Reception in the Eighteenth-Century British Press and Laurence Sterne
Mary Newbould

A full series listing is available at: www.cambridge.org/EECC

Printed by Integrated Books International,
United States of America